Project Censored Guide to Independent Media and Activism

D1714438

Project Censored Guide to Independent Media and Activism

Peter Phillips and Project Censored

AN OPEN MEDIA BOOK

SEVEN STORIES PRESS
New York

In Canada: Hushion House, 36 Northline Road, Toronto, Ontario M4B 3E2

In the U.K.: Turnaround Publisher Services Ltd., Unit 3, Olympia Trading Estate, Coburg Road, Wood Green, London N22 6TZ

In Australia: Palgrave Macmillan, 627 Chapel Street, South Yarra, VIC 3141

Cover design: Greg Ruggiero

Front cover: Kobie Maitland inside the Seattle IMC, November 1999, as protesters filled the streets outside. © Greg Ruggiero

Back cover: November 17, 1999 Seattle. © Greg Ruggiero

ISBN: 1-58322-468-8

Printed in Canada.

9 8 7 6 5 4 3 2 1

CONTENTS

ACKNOWLEDGEMENTS

The principal researcher for this guide was Katie Sims, a long-time Project Censored activist and dedicated staff member. She spent hundreds of hours working on this guide over the past two years. In addition to this work, Katie is the central person who coordinates the story management process at Project Censored.

Special thanks to Sonoma State University Project Censored interns: Emily Oberg, Odilia Pablo, Sarah Potts, Karen Torres-Valle, Jaleah Winn, Jonetta Woods and all the interns/community volunteers who made this resource possible.

INTRODUCTION

The Importance of Independent News Sources for Freedom and Democracy

BY PETER PHILLIPS

Since the passage of the Telecommunications Act of 1996, a gold rush of media mergers and takeovers has occurred in the United States. More than half of all radio stations have been sold in the past six years, and the repeatedly merged AOL–Time-Warner (CNN) is the largest media organization in the world. Fewer than ten major media corporations dominate U.S. news and information systems. Clear Channel owns More than 1,200 radio stations. Ninety-eight percent of all cities have only one daily newspaper and these are increasingly owned by huge chains like Gannett and Knight-Ridder. In medicine it is called Managed Care—in media it's Managed News. Corporate media today are in the entertainment business. Market share, advertising dollars, and political self-interest drive the corporate media agenda.

Lost to society is a diversity of political viewpoints and news story sources that are so important for democracy and freedom. We can see this quite clearly in the news coverage after the 9/11 attacks. Media's criticism of the government has become unpatriotic. The corporate media's line reads more like a government press release than a free society's analysis of important events of the day. We cannot have an active democracy with a news system that self-censors stories based on their political acceptability or marketability ratings rather than considering the importance of the news story for maintaining an informed electorate

We need to rethink our systems of news and information. Imagine having hundreds of independent news sources in society. Imagine real news that builds democracy and freedom—news that contributes to the lives and sociopolitical understandings of a vast majority of the people. Real news could inform and awaken the less powerful in society. Real news would not be measured with Arbitron ratings. It would not exist for the selling of materialism. Real news would be measured through its success in building democracy and stimulating grassroots activism. Real news would speak truth to power and would challenge the hegemonic top-down corporate propaganda-laden news system. Real news would empower and keep key segments of working people in America tuned in, informed, and active. Real news would build movements for social change. It would help keep progressive activists aware of their power and collective ability to influence positive change. Real news would stimulate social activism and organize movement toward betterment, shape policy for equality, and stand in the face of robber-baron power brokers everywhere.

Independent real-news media come from the people, and are emerging around us. Independent newsmagazines, newspapers, local cable-TV access, independent radio, and micro-transmitted radio are everywhere. Independent media offer a vast diversity of news and information and are expanding daily. The new Indymedia activists alone now have direct links to more than one hundred grassroots news sites around the world. Most of the independent news sources listed in this resource guide are willing to share stories with local publications for reprinting and broadcast if full credit is given. The challenge is to make these news sources widely available to the majority of working people in our society. We must find ways to compile, sort, and collectively release real news to millions of people. Media activist news groups like the Asheville Global Report and the North Bay Progressive are building local newspapers that summarize and consolidate real news for thousands of people. With the Internet there is a great potential for thousands of interconnected small local newspapers, independent radio broadcasters, and TV stations to eventually rival the monopoly of the corporate media conglomerates. We can build from the bottom up and reawaken the democratic spirit of our society. We can add to, and expand, the vital sources of real news listed in this resource guide. We can tell our stories of struggling and overcoming together, and those stories will strengthen and build grassroots democracy and freedom.

OUR FAVORITE WEB SITES

ABYA YALA NEWS: ONLINE
P.O. Box 7829
Oakland, CA 94601
(510) 534-4882
indian@igc.org
www.saiic.nativeweb.org/ayn

An exclusively online journal which presents a unique source of news and analysis relating to indigenous issues in Meso and South America from indigenous peoples' perspectives. The journal works to raise international awareness on issues of indigenous autonomy and self-development and also to facilitate the formation of alliances among the native people of Latin America.

ALTERNET
Institute for Alternative Journalism
77 Federal St.
San Francisco, CA 94107
(415) 284-1420
Fax: (415) 284-1414
info@alternet.org
www.alternet.org

A news service for the alternative press, IAJ supports independent and alternative journalism.

AMERICAN DISPATCHES
2200 Wilson Blvd. Suite 102-231
Arlington, VA 20001
amdispatches@aol.com
www.americandispatches.com

As both the old-fashioned print industry and the high-tech Internet news sites are overwhelmed by mega-media corporations, we hope our joint print-Web publication, American Dispatches and americandispatches.com, can point to a different—and more independent—path for online and print journalism.

BLACKPRESSUSA.COM
2711 East 75th Place
Chicago, IL 60649
(312) 375-8200
Fax: (312) 375-8262
info@blackpressusa.com
www.blackpressusa.com/aboutus/ab
outus.asp

BlackPressUSA.com is the joint Web presence of America's black community newspapers and the NNPA News Service—the last national black-press news wire. It is a project of the Black Press Institute, a partnership between the National Newspaper Publishers Association Foundation and Howard University: "Your independent source of news for the African-American community."

BLUE EAR

www.blueear.com

Blue Ear is an editorial partnership publishing international journalism and writing in a variety of digital formats.

CENTRE FOR RESEARCH ON GLOBALIZATION

www.globalresearch.ca

The Centre for Research on Globalization (CRG) is an independent research and media group of progressive writers, scholars and activists committed tocurbing the tide of "globalization" and "disarming" the New World Order.

COMMON DREAMS

P.O. Box 443
Portland, ME 04112-0443
(207) 799-2185
Fax: (619) 798-6341
editor@commondreams.org
www.commondreams.org

A national nonprofit, grassroots organization whose mission is to organize an open, honest and non-partisan national discussion of current events. The Web site is one of the best organized on national and international topics.

CONSORTIUM FOR INDEPENDENT JOURNALISM, THE

2200 Wilson Blvd., Suite 102-231
Arlington, VA 22201
(703) 920-1580
Fax: (703) 920-0946
consortnew@aol.com
www.consortiumnews.com

An independent investigative news company.

CORPWATCH

P.O. Box 29344
San Francisco, CA 94129
(415) 561-6568
Fax: (415) 561-6493
corpwatch@corpwatch.org
www.corpwatch.org

CorpWatch counters corporate-led globalization through education and activism. They work to foster democratic control over corporations by building grassroots globalization—a diverse movement for human rights, labor rights and environmental justice.

DAILY BRIEFING

1900 M Street, Suite 210
Washington, DC 20036
(202) 293-7394
Fax: (202) 293-6946
info@journalism.org
www.journalism.org/daily/index.html

Daily news briefing put out by the Project for Excellence in Journalism.

DAILY MEDIA NEWS

1600 Broadway Suite 700
New York, NY 10019
(212) 246-0202
Fax: (212) 246-2677
www.medicachannel.org/nws/today/index.html

Mediachannel's international roundup of breaking stories about the media.

DATA LOUNGE

editorial@datalounge.com
www.datalounge.com

Web site with news focus on national and international gay/lesbian issues.

DEMOCRACY NOW!

WBAI
120 Wall St., 10th Floor
New York, NY 10005
(212) 397-0886
mail@democracynow.org
www.democracynow.org

Democracy Now! was launched by Pacifica Radio in 1996 to open the airwaves on a daily basis to alternative voices traditionally excluded from the political process. Programs with host Amy Goodman are now available online.

ENVIROLINK NETWORK

5801 Beacon St. Suite #2
Pittsburgh, PA 15217
support@envirolink.org
http://envirolink.netforchange.com
One of the world's largest environmental information clearinghouses, EnviroLink also provides environmental and animal rights nonprofit organizations with free Internet services.

ENVIRONMENTAL MEDIA SERVICES

1320 18th Street NW, 2nd Floor
Washington, DC 20036
(202) 463-6670
Fax: (202) 463-6671
www.ems.org

EMS is a nonprofit communications clearinghouse dedicated to expanding media coverage of critical environmental and public health issues.

ENVIRONMENTAL NEWS SERVICE
(800) 632-9528
news@ens-news.com
http://ens.lycos.com

ENS is a newswire for environmental issues.

EYE MAGAZINE
P.O. Box 9145
Greensboro, NC 27429-0145
(910) 370-1702
Fax: (910) 370-1603
info@eyemag.com
www.eyemag.com

A forum for underreported news, Eye Magazine is also a watchdog for coverups and scandals in corporate America.

FACULTY ACTIVIST DIRECTORY, THE
Teachers for a Democratic Culture
Temple University English Dept.
Philadelphia, PA 19122
sparkss@astro.ocis.temple.edu
www.tdc2000.org/fad/index.html

A Web-based directory of progressive faculty organizations, disciplinary-based caucuses, academic programs, and listserve discussion groups, the directory aims to create a common site where individuals can learn about progressive activities being done in their school, their community, or their discipline. Any socially or politically progressive organization or program is welcome to post on this site.

FREE SPEECH TV
P.O. Box 6060
Boulder, CO 80306
(303) 442-8445
Fax: (303) 442-6472
Programming@sftv.org
www.freespeech.org

A progressive voice in the media revolution, Free Speech TV brings activist and alternative media into seven million homes each week.

GLOBAL ISSUES
comments@globalissues.org
www.globalissues.org

This Web site looks into global issues that affect everyone and aims to show how most issues are interrelated. Global Issues features over 3000 links to external articles, Web sites, reports and analysis.

GLOBAL SPIN
goto@globalspin.org
www.globalspin.org

GlobalSpin offers "News & Views from Abroad" and is dedicated to bringing more of those voices to you. It is a door to the thoughts and opinions of vast segments of the world outside the American media empire.

GUERRILLA NEWS NETWORK

www.GuerrillaNews.com

Guerrilla News Network is an underground news organization based in New York City and Berkeley, California. They expose important global issues through guerrilla programming.

HOME TOWN ADVANTAGE BULLETIN, THE

1313 5th Street SE
Minneapolis, MN 55414
(612) 379-3815
Fax: (612) 379-3920
home_town_advantage-subscribe@topica.com
www.newrules.org/hta/index.htm

Published by the Institute for Local Self-Reliance, the Hometown Advantage Bulletin is a bimonthly electronic newsletter reporting on efforts nationwide to stop chain store proliferation and support locally owned, independent retail businesses. Learn about land use policies and other tools that can protect the character and vitality of your hometown. Find out how other communities are bucking the "big box" retail trend and encouraging small-scale, homegrown businesses—and why this approach is proving far more beneficial to the local economy.

INDEPENDENT MEDIA CENTER

general@indymedia.org
www.indymedia.org

The Independent Media Center is a network of collectively run media outlets for the creation of radical, accurate and passionate tellings of the truth. "We work out of a love for and inspiration by people who continue to work for a better world, despite corporate media's distortions and unwillingness to cover the efforts to free humanity." Founded in 1999 in an effort to cover the anti–WTO protests in Seattle, IMCs have since sprouted up in dozens of regions around the world, from Chiapas to Jerusalem. Providing free media access online, IMC is an invaluable resource.

INEQUALITY.ORG

(212) 894-3704 x2487
info@Inequality.org
www.Inequality.org

News, information and expertise on the divide in income, wealth and health.

INTERNATIONAL ACTION CENTER

(212) 633-6646
Fax: (212) 633-2889
39 West 14th Street
New York, NY 10011
iacenter@action-mail.org
www.iacenter.org

Social activism organization founded by Ramsey Clark, former U.S.
Attorney General.

IPS (INTER PRESS SERVICE)

online@ips.org
www.ips.org

Inter Press Service, the world's leading provider of information on global issues, is backed by a network of
journalists in more than 100 countries, with satellite communication
links to 1,200 outlets. IPS focuses
its news coverage on the events and
global processes affecting the economic, social and political development of peoples and nations.

LABOR BEAT

37 S Ashland Blvd., Suite W
Chicago, IL 60607
(312) 226-3330
Fax: (773) 561-0908
laborbeat@fs.freespeech.org
http://myweb.wwa.com/~bgfolder/lb

An independent rank-and-file labor
forum, Labor Beat produces labor

television and radio, advocates for
labor media and is the voice of
Labor issues in today's news. Labor
Beat's Web site offers selected links
on labor and media issues.

LIP MAGAZINE

1400 West Devon Ave., #136
Chicago, IL 60660
(312) 458-9123
info@lipmagazine.org
www.lipmagazine.org

A not-for-profit electronic (and soon
to be print) media project, Lip is
dedicated to building a sustainable
society that values diversity. "We
question public and private policy
that confuses consumption with
freedom and ignores the human
costs of rote and mind-numbing
work and pursues the destruction of
the natural environment." Lip is the
proud porovider of "Media
Dissidence & Uncivil Discourse
Since 1996."

MEDIACHANNEL

1600 Broadway, #700
New York, NY 10019
editor@mediachannel.org
www.mediachannel.org

The Web site produced by
Globalvision New Media,
Mediachannel is an online global
media supersite.

MICHAEL MOORE

www.michaelmoore.com/

Michael Moore's Web page for activists and news.

MISC. ACTIVISM PROGRESSIVE

map@pencil.cs.missouri.edu
webmap.missouri.edu

A moderate Internet news group concerned with human rights, empowerment and democracy, with a worldwide readership.

MODEL MINORITY

modelminority@email.com
www.modelminority.com

This site is your guide to Asian-American empowerment.

MOTHERJONES.COM/MOJO WIRE

www.motherjones.com/about_us

MotherJones.com's guide to under-covered news, commentary and resources.

PACIFIC NEWS SERVICE

660 Market St.
San Francisco, CA 94104
(415)438-4755
www.pacificnews.org

Produces daily progressive new stories for publication.

PEACE AND JUSTICE CENTER (PALO ALTO)

457 Kingsley Ave.
Palo Alto, CA 94301
(650) 326-8837
www.peaceandjustice.org

This site features hundreds of great links to independent news and sources.

PRIME-NEWS AGENCY

5 Kutateladze Turn
Tbilisi, Georgia
(99532) 92 32 12, 92 32 14
Fax: (99532) 92 32 02
pna@pna.com.ge
www.prime-news.com.ge

Prime News Agency (PNA) is a fully independent news-gathering organization with its headquarters in Tbilisi, Georgia reporting all the news from the Caucasus region.

PROGRESSIVE RESPONSE

newusfp-subscribe@lists.zianet.com
www.foreignpolicy-infocus.org/

This site, the e-journal of Foreign Policy In Focus is "Working to make the U.S. a more responsible global leader and partner."

RADIO FOR ALL

radio4all@radio4all
www.radio4all.org

Providing global links to alternative free radio, Radio For All is the hub Web site for the U.S. micro-radio movement with links to clandestine stations, support groups, news and announcements, policy updates, legal information, and detailed primers on how to start a new station.

RUCKUS SOCIETY, THE

www.ruckus.org/about/index.html

The is the site of the Ruckus Society, a group working with a broad range of communities, organizations, and movements to change our relationship with the environment and each other.

SALON

22 4th Street, 16th Floor
San Francisco, CA 94103
(415) 645-9200
Fax: (415) 645-9204
dtalbot@salon.com
www.salon.com

Founded in November 1995 by David Talbot, Salon.com is an Internet media company that produces ten original content sites as well as two online communities—Table Talk and The WELL. The content sites, updated daily or more fre-

quently, include News, Politics, Technology & Business, Arts & Entertainment, Books and more.

SAN FRANCISCO BAY AREA PROGRESSIVE DIRECTORY

P.O. Box 11232
Berkeley, CA 94712-2232
(510) 843-9521
cheetham@igc.org
bapd.org/dirinfo.html

A directory of about 1,000 nonprofit and activist organizations in the counties surrounding the San Francisco Bay, with additional links to other progressive sites elsewhere.

TALK LEFT

talkleft@aol.com
www.talkleft.com

The online source for liberal coverage of crime-related political and injustice news.

TAO COMMUNICATIONS

TAO Toronto
P.O. Box 108, Station P
Toronto, ON M5S 2S8
Canada
(416) 812-6765
ao-www@tao.ca
www.tao.ca

A Canada-based federation comprised of local autonomous collectives and individuals, Tao organizes networks in order to defend and expand public space and the right to self-determination and is host to an array of online movement networks and Web sites.

TOMPAINE.COMMONSENSE
www.tompaine.com

This "Journal of Opinion" seeks to enrich the national debate on controversial public issues by featuring the ideas opinions, and analyses too often overlooked by the mainstream media. We promote these in our weekly advertisement on the op-ed page of the New York Times.

TRUTHOUT.COM
767 South San Perdo St.
Los Angeles, CA 90014
comments@truthout.com
www.truthout.com

An independent forum for investigative articles and editorials.

UNITED FOR A FAIR ECONOMY
37 Temple Place, 2nd Floor
Boston, MA 02111
(617) 423-2148
Fax: (617) 423-0191
info@faireconomy.org

United for a Fair Economy was founded as a "movement support" organization to provide media capacity, face-to-face economic literacy education, and training resources to organizations and individuals who work to address the widening income and asset gap in the United States.

WORLD SOCIALIST WEBSITE
Editor@wsws.org
www.wsws.org

The World Socialist Website is the online hub for the International Committee of the Fourth International (ICFI). It provides analysis of major world events, comments on political, cultural, historical and philosophical issues, and valuable documents and studies from the heritage of the socialist movement.

ZENZIBAR NEWS SERVICE
dreamers@zenzibar.com
zenzibar.com/news/newsarchive.asp

Zenzibar Alternative Culture is a portal to, and directory of alternatives to Western mainstream culture.

ZNET
18 Millfield St.
Woods Hole, MA 02543
www.zmag.weluser.htm

Z Magazine's news and links.

ORGANIZATIONS

ABORIGINAL MULTI-MEDIA SOCIETY, THE (AMMSA)
15001-112th Avenue
Edmonton, AB T5M 2V6
Canada
(780) 455-2700
Fax: (780) 455-7639
market@ammsa.com
www.ammsa.com/ammsa.html

Through print and electronic media AMMSA provides a forum for the exchange of information about cultural issues and events in Native communities.

ADVOCATES FOR YOUTH
1025 Vermont Ave. NW, Suite 200
Washington, DC 20005
(202) 347-5700
Fax: (202) 347-2263
info@advocatesforyouth.org
www.advocatesforyouth.org

Advocates seeks to support and educate teens and adolescents regarding sexuality, reproduction and sexually transmitted diseases.

A-INFOS NEWS SERVICE
a-infos-org@ainfos.ca
www.ainfos.ca

The A-Infos Project is coordinated by an international collective of revolutionary, anti-authoritarian, anti-capitalist activists involved with class struggle.

ALLAFRICA GLOBAL MEDIA
920 M Street SE
Washington, DC 27702
(202) 546-0777
Fax: (202) 546-0676.
info@allafrica.com
allafrica.com

Disseminates stories from African news organizations.

ALLIANCE FOR COMMUNITY MEDIA
666 11th Street NW, Suite 740
Washington, DC 20001-4542
(202) 393-2650 x1
acm@alliancecm.org
www.alliancecm.org

The Alliance for Community Media is committed to ensuring everyone's access to electronic media through public education, a progressive legislative and regulatory agenda, coalition building and grassroots organizing.

ALLIANCE FOR CULTURAL DEMOCRACY
P.O. Box 192244
San Francisco, CA 94119-2244
(415) 821-9652 and (415) 437-2721
Fax: (718) 488-8296
ACD@f8.com/ACD/
www.f8.com/ACD

Alliance for Cultural Democracy is a 25-year-old international organization and network of community and cultural activists working on a wide range of community arts, education and cultural activism.

ALLSTON-BRIGHTON FREE RADIO
c/o Steve Provizer
23 Winslow Rd.
Brookline, MA 02146
(617) 232-3174
www.radfrall.org

This group seeks out the most politically and culturally disenfranchised citizens and community groups and provides them with the tools necessary to both access mainstream media and to create alternative media outlets.

ALTERNATIVE PRESS INDEX
P.O. Box 33109
Baltimore, MD 21218
(410) 243-2471
Fax: (410) 235-5325
altpress@altpress.org
www.altpress.org

Alternative Press Center co-publishes the Alternative Press Index and Annotations (a guide to independent critical press), and also maintains a library.

ALTERNATIVES IN PRINT TASK FORCE
Office of Literacy and Outreach Services, American Library Association
P.O. Box 720511
San Jose, CA 95172
(312) 280-4295
aip@libr.org
libr.org/AIP

This group advocates local selection and cataloging of materials from small and alternative presses and independent producers by sponsoring programs and Internet discussions; linking grassroots groups; and publishing reviews, articles, exhibits, online resources, the biennial directory Alternative Publishers of Books in North America (CRISES Press) and more.

AMERICAN CIVIL LIBERTIES UNION (ACLU)

125 Broad St., 18th Floor
New York, NY 10004-2400
(212) 549-2500
Fax: (212) 549-2646
aclu@aclu.org
www.aclu.org

The ACLU provides information regarding issues of civil liberties, including online information on Internet free speech issues.

AMERICAN FRIENDS SERVICE COMMITTEE (AFSC)

1501 Cherry St.
Philadelphia, PA 19102
(215) 241-7000
Fax: (215) 241-7275
afscinfo@afsc.org
www.afsc.org

Founded in 1917, AFSC is a national Quaker organization that includes people of various faiths dedicated to humanitarian service, reconciliation, peace and social justice issues.

AMERICAN HELLENIC MEDIA PROJECT

P.O. Box 1150
New York, NY 10028-0008
ahmp@hri.org
www.hri.org/ahmp

AHMP is a grassroots, not-for-profit think tank created to educate the media regarding American-Hellenic issues and to further address the increasingly anti-Hellenic posture of our nation's press and media establishment.

AMERICAN LIBRARY ASSOCIATION OFFICE FOR INTELLECTUAL FREEDOM

50 E Huron St.
Chicago, IL 60611
(312) 280-4223 and (800) 545-2433
Fax: (312) 280-4227
oif@ala.org
www.ala.org/oif.html

Organized to educate librarians and the general public about the nature and importance of intellectual freedom in libraries.

AMERICAN SOCIETY OF JOURNALISTS AND AUTHORS

1501 Broadway, Suite. 302
New York, NY 10036
(212) 997-0947
Fax: (212) 768-7414
102535.2427@compuserve.com
www.asja.org

The Society produces a membership directory listing 1000 nonfiction freelance writers, their coordinates and writing specialties.

AMERICAN SOCIETY OF NEWSPAPER EDITORS (ASNE)
11690-B Sunrise Valley Dr.
Reston, VA 20191-1409
(703) 456-1122
Fax: (703) 453-1133
asne@asne.org
www.asne.org

ASNE discusses topics related to the current state and future of newspapers and journalism in this country.

AMNESTY INTERNATIONAL
322 8th Avenue
New York, NY 10001
(212) 807-8400
Fax: (212) 463-9193 and (212) 627-1451
admin-us@aiusa.org
membership: aimember@aiusa.org
www.amnesty.org

AI is an international organization that works to ensure human rights throughout the world, and oppose and document human rights violations.

APPLIED RESEARCH CENTER
3781 Broadway
Oakland, CA 94611
(510) 653-3415
Fax: (510) 653-3427
arc@arc.org
www.arc.org

A public policy, education and research institute that emphasizes issues of race and social change, ARC is the publisher of Colorlines.

ASIAN AMERICAN JOURNALISTS ASSOCIATION (AAJA)
1182 Market St., Suite 320
San Francisco, CA 94102
(415) 346-2051
Fax: (415) 346-6343
national@aaja.org
www.aaja.org

AAJA is committed to insuring diversity in American journalism and expressing the Asian-American perspective.

ASSOCIATION OF ALTERNATIVE NEWSWEEKLIES
1020 16th Street NW, 4th Floor
Washington, DC 20036-5702
(202) 822-1955
Fax: (202) 822-0929
ann@aan.org
aan.org

A coordinating and administrative organization for 113 alternative newsweeklies in the U.S. and Canada.

ASSOCIATION OF AMERICAN PUBLISHERS (AAP)
71 5th Avenue
New York, NY 10003-3004
(212) 255-0200
Fax: (212) 255-7007
amyg@publishers.org
www.publishers.org

The Association of American Publishers (AAP), with some 310 members located throughout the United States, is the principal trade association of the book publishing industry.

BERKELEY MEDIA STUDIES GROUP
2140 Shattuck Ave., Suite 804
Berkeley, CA 94704
(510) 204-9700
Fax: (510) 204-9710
bmsg@bmsg.org

This journalism and media research group at UC Berkeley has a Web site forthcoming in 2002.

BEYOND MEDIA, INC.
6960 N Sheridan Rd., Store B
Chicago, IL 60626
(773) 973-2280
Fax: (773) 973-3367
beyond@beyondmedia.org
www.beyondmedia.org

A nonprofit organization dedicated to creating alternative media for positive social change, Beyond Media specializes in video production and other media arts and outreach campaigns. Centering the programs and stories of specific women and girls within the framework of transcultural issues, the program constructs bridges across which members of widely diverse communities can work together and educate one another.

BLACK PRESS INSTITUTE
2711 East 75th Place
Chicago, IL 60649
(312) 375-8200
Fax: (312) 375-8262
info@blackpressusa.com
www.blackpressusa.com/aboutus/ab
outus.asp

A partnership between the National Newspaper Publishers Association Foundation (NNPAF) and Howard University, the Institute provides an academic link to the black press, coordinating national internship, fellowship and scholarship programs and creating innovative programs designed to help close the digital media divide.

BLACK WOMEN IN PUBLISHING
P.O. Box 6275, FDR Station
New York, NY 10150
(212) 772-5951
bwip@hotmail.com
www.bwip.org

Black Women In Publishing, Inc.
(BWIP) is an employee-based trade
association dedicated both to
increasing the presence, and supporting the efforts, of African-her-
itage women and men in the publishing industry.

**CALIFORNIA FIRST
AMENDMENT COALITION**
2701 Cottage Way, Suite 12
Sacramento, CA 95825-1226
(916) 974-8888
Fax: (916) 974-8880
cfac@cfac.org
http://cfac.org

**CAMPUS ALTERNATIVE
JOURNALISM PROJECT**
Center for Campus Organizing
P.O. Box 425748
Cambridge, MA 02142
(415) 643-4401
Fax: (617) 547-5067
cajp@indypress.org
www.indypress.org/programs/cajp.html

CAPJ supports the work of progressive campus print-media activists.
We provide resource guides, train-
ings and consultation, and organize
a network of over 100 publications.

**CENTER FOR COMMERCIAL-
FREE PUBLIC EDUCATION, THE**
1714 Franklin St., Suite # 101-306
Oakland, CA 94612
(510) 268-1100
Fax: (510) 268-1277
unplug@igc.org

www.commercialfree.org
The Center for Commercial-Free
Public Education, home of the
Unplug Campaign, is a national
nonprofit organization that addresses the issue of commercialism in
our public schools. The Center provides support to students, parents,
teachers and other concerned citizens organizing across the U.S. to
keep their schools commercial free
and community controlled.

**CENTER FOR CONSTITUTIONAL
RIGHTS (CCR)**
666 Broadway, 7th Floor
New York, NY 10012
(212) 614-6464
Fax: (212) 614-6499
info@ccr-ny.org
www.ccr-ny.org

The Center for Constitutional
Rights (CCR) is a non-profit legal
and educational organization dedicated to protecting and advancing
the rights guaranteed by the U.S.
Constitution and the Universal
Declaration of Human Rights.

CENTER FOR DEFENSE INFORMATION (CDI)

1779 Massachusetts Ave. NW
Washington, DC 20036
(202) 332-0600
Fax: (202) 462-4559
info@cdi.org
www.cdi.org

CDI opposes excessive military expenditures that increase the dangers of war. CDI believes that social, economic, political and environmental factors contribute as much to a nation's security as does a strong military defense.

CENTER FOR DEMOCRACY AND TECHNOLOGY, THE

1634 Eye St. NW, Suite 1100
Washington, DC 20006
(202) 637-9800
Fax: (202) 637-0968
feedback@cdt.org
www.cdt.org

The Center for Democracy and Technology works to promote freedom of speech, democratic values and constitutional liberties in the digital age. With expertise in law, technology, and policy, CDT seeks practical solutions to enhance free expression and privacy in global communications technologies.

CENTER FOR DEMOCRATIC COMMUNICATIONS OF THE NATIONAL LAWYERS GUILD, THE

240 Stockton St., 3rd Floor
San Francisco, CA 94108
(415) 522-9814
Fax: (415) 381-9963
cdc@nlg.org
www.nlgcdc.org

The Center focuses on the right of all peoples to have access to a world-wide system of media and communications with the principle of cultural and informational self-determination. This committee is an important force in micro-radio advocacy and activism.

CENTER FOR HEALTH, ENVIRONMENT & JUSTICE (CHEJ)

P.O. Box 6806
Falls Church, VA 22046-6806
(703) 237-2249
Fax: (703) 237-8389
chej@chej.org
www.chej.org

A 20-year-old nonprofit, grassroots organization providing scientific, organizing and technical assistance to citizens concerned with dioxin, toxic waste and chemical toxins in their communities, CHEJ is also the publisher of two periodicals: Everyone's Backyard and Environmental Health Monthly.

CENTER FOR INTERNATIONAL POLICY (CIP)
1755 Massachusetts Ave. NW, Suite 550
Washington, DC 20036
(202) 232-3317
Fax: (202) 232-3440
cip@ciponline.org
www.us.net/cip

CIP promotes a U.S. foreign policy that reflects democratic values. Its programs include the Demilitarization Program, to reduce the size and role of the military in Central America, and the Intelligence Reform Program, to reexamine and reform the U.S. intelligence community.

CENTER FOR INVESTIGATIVE REPORTING
500 Howard St., Suite 206
San Francisco, CA 94105-3000
(415) 543-1200
Fax: (415) 543-8311
CIR@igc.org
www.muckraker.org/pubs/paper-trails/index.html

CENTER FOR MEDIA AND PUBLIC AFFAIRS
2100 L Street NW, Suite 300
Washington, DC 20037
(202) 223-2942
Fax: (202) 872-4014
www.cmpa.com/html/2100.html

CENTER FOR MEDIA EDUCATION
2120 L Street, NW Suite 200
Washington, DC 20037
(202) 331-7833
Fax: (202) 331-7841
cme@cme.org
www.cme.org

Formerly the publishers of InfoActive Kids, the Center For Media Education focuses on child advocacy, consumer, health and educational communities and is a resource for journalists covering children and media topics.

CENTER FOR MEDIA LITERACY
4727 Wilshire Blvd., Suite #403
Los Angeles, CA 90010
(213) 931-4177 and (800) 226-9494
Fax: (213) 931-4474
cml@medialit.org
www.medialit.org

The Center for Media Literacy is a nonprofit educational organization that provides leadership, professional development, and educational resources. Dedicated to providing and supporting media literary education as a framework for accessing, analyzing, evaluating, and creating media content, CML works to help people develop their critical thinking and media production skills.

CENTER FOR PUBLIC INTEGRITY

910 17th Street NW, 7th Floor
Washington, DC 20006
(202) 466-1300
Fax: (202) 466-1101
contact@publicintegrity.org
www.publicintegrity.org

The CPI provides a mechanism through which important national issues can be analyzed by responsible journalists and the results published in full form without traditional time and space limitations. The CPI is the publisher of The Public I.

CENTER FOR RESPONSIVE POLITICS

1101 14th Street NW, Suite 1030
Washington, DC 2005-5635
(202) 857-0044
Fax: (202) 857-7809
info@crp.org
www.opensecrets.org

The CRP is a nonpartisan, nonprofit research group that specializes in the study of Congress, particularly the role that money plays in its elections and actions. The Center's work is aimed at creating a more involved citizenry and a more responsive Congress.

CENTER FOR SCIENCE IN THE PUBLIC INTEREST

1875 Connecticut Ave. NW, Suite 300
Washington, DC 20009
(202) 332-9110
Fax: (202) 265-4954
cspi@cspinet.org
www.cspinet.org

Dedicated to supporting science and scientists who actively participate in promoting the public interest and general welfare, the Center for Science in the Public Interest publishes the Nutrition Action Healthletter.

CENTER FOR THIRD WORLD ORGANIZING (CTWO)

1218 East 21st Street
Oakland, CA 94606
(510) 533-7583
Fax: (510) 533-0923
ctwo@ctwo.org
www.ctwo.org

CTWO is a national racial justice movement hub that works with individuals and organizations to craft political analysis, organizing skills and visions of a just society.

CENTER OF CONCERN (COC)

1225 Otis St. NE
Washington, DC 20017
(202) 635-2757
Fax: (202) 832-9494
coc@coc.org
www.coc.org

This independent, interdisciplinary organization is engaged in social analysis, theological reflection, policy advocacy and public education on issues of development, peace and justice.

CHICAGO MEDIA WATCH

P.O. Box 268737
Chicago, IL 60626
(773) 604-1910
cmw@mediawatch.org
www.mediawatch.org/~cmw

CISPES (COMMITTEE IN SOLIDARITY WITH THE PEOPLE OF EL SALVADOR)

P.O. Box 1801
New York, NY 10159
(212) 465-8115
Fax: (212) 465-8998
cispesnatl@people-link.net
cispes.org

CISPES are th publishers of El Salvador Watch, a newsletter following the continuing struggle of popular Salvadoran political, labor and women's movements, and spotlighting CISPES' programming and organizing work throughout the United States.

CITIZENS FOR INDEPENDENT PUBLIC BROADCASTING

901 Old Hickory Rd.
Pittsburg, PA 15243
(412) 341-1967
Fax: (412) 341-6533
jmstarr@cais.com
www.cipbonline.org

This citizens group coordinates a national education campaign to reform public broadcasting as a public trust, independent of government and corporate control, and encourages community groups to democratize their local public broadcasting stations.

CITIZENS FOR MEDIA LITERACY

34 Wall St., Suite 407
Asheville, NC 28801
(828) 255-0182
Fax: (828) 254-2286
cml@main.nc.us
www.main.nc.us/cml

CIVIC MEDIA CENTER & LIBRARY, INC.
1021 W University Ave.
Gainsville, FL 32601
(352) 373-0010
coordinator@civicmediacenter.org
www.civicmediacenter.org

A nonprofit library and reading room of alternative press publications, the facility contains books, periodicals, reference materials (including the Alternative Press Index), an E-'zine library, and an audio and video collection.

COLLISION COURSE VIDEO PRODUCTIONS
P.O. Box 347383
San Francisco, CA 94134-7383
(415) 587-0818
Fax: (415) 587-0818
video@collissioncourse.com
www.bapd.org/kfi-eo-1.html

Collision creates and distributes activist videos on anti-interventionism, police abuse, abortion rights and indigenous issues. They are the producers of the educational video "Viva La Casa! 500 Years of Chicano History" and two youth-oriented monthly cable TV programs.

COMMITTEE TO PROTECT JOURNALISTS
330 7th Aveue, 12th Floor
New York, NY 10001
(212) 465-1004
Fax: (212) 465-9568
Info@cpj.org
www.cpj.org

The Committee to Protect Journalists, dedicated to safeguarding journalists and freedom of expression worldwide, is a nonprofit, nonpartisan organization that monitors abuses of the press and promotes press freedom internationally.

COMMON CAUSE
1250 Connecticut Ave, NW, #600
Washington, DC, MD 20036
(202) 833-1200
Fax: (202) 659-3716
grassroots@commoncouse.org
www.commoncause.org

Common Cause supports open, accountable government and the right of all American citizens to be involved in shaping the nation's public policies. Particularly, it presses for the enactment of campaign finance reform.

COMMUNITY MEDIA WORKSHOP

Columbia College
600 S Michigan Ave.
Chicago, IL 60605-1996
(312) 344-6400
Fax: (312) 344-6404
Cmw@newstips.org
www.newstips.org

CMW trains community organizations and civic groups to use media more effectively and helps journalists learn of their stories. They are the publishers of Getting on the Air & Into Print!, a 200-page citizen's guide to media in the Chicago area.

CONSUMER PROJECT ON TECHNOLOGY

P.O. Box 19367
Washington, DC 20036
(202)387-8030
Fax: (202) 234-5176
love@cptech.org
www.cptech.org

CPT is active in a number of areas, including intellectual property, telecommunications and privacy and electronic commerce. It has developed a variety of projects relating to antitrust enforcement and policy.

CONSUMER'S UNION OF UNITED STATES, INC.

101 Truman Ave.
Yonkers, NY 10703-1057
(914) 378-2000
Fax: (914) 378-2900
www. consumersunion.org

Consumers Union, publisher of Consumer Reports, advances the interests of consumers by providing information and advice about products and services, and advocating on consumers' behalf.

CO-OP AMERICA

1612 K Street NW, Suite 600
Washington, DC 20006
(800) 58-GREEN and (202) 872-5307
Fax: (202) 331-8166
info@coopamerica.org
www.coopamerica.org

A national nonprofit organization founded in 1982, Co-op America is the leading force in educating and empowering people and businesses to make significant improvements through the economic system. They are the publishers of National Green Pages and Co-op America Quarterly.

COUNCIL FOR A LIVABLE WORLD

110 Maryland Ave. NE
Washington, DC 20002
(202) 543-4100
Fax: (202) 543-6297
clw@clw.org
www.clw.org

Founded in 1962, the Council supports political candidates who support deep military reductions and elimination of nuclear weapons. Its mission is to eliminate all weapons of mass destruction.

COUNCIL OF CANADIANS

502-151 Slater St.
Ottawa, ON K1P 5H3
Canada
(613) 233-2773
Fax: (613) 233-6776
www.canadians.org

The Council of Canadians is Canada's pre-eminent citizens' watchdog organization, comprised of over 100,000 members and more than 70 chapters across the country. Strictly non-partisan, it lobbies members of Parliament, conducts research, and runs national campaigns spotlighting the nation's most pressing issues.

COUNCIL ON INTERNATIONAL AND PUBLIC AFFAIRS (CIPA)

P.O. Box 246
S Yarmouth, MA 02664-0246
(508) 398-1145
Fax: (508) 398-1552
people@poclad.org
www.poclad.org

Instigating democratic conversations and actions that contest the authority of corporations to govern, the Council also publishes Program On Corporations, Law & Democracy.

DOWNTOWN COMMUNITY TV CENTER

87 Lafayette St.
New York, NY 10013
(212) 966-4510
Fax: (212) 219-0248
Web@dctvny.org
www.dctvny.org

Founded in 1972, DCTV believes that expanding public access to the electronic media arts invigorates our democracy. DCTV pursues a grassroots mission to teach people, particularly members of low-income and minority communites, how to use media.

EARTH FIRST!
P.O. Box 1415
Eugene, OR 97440
(541) 344-8004
Fax: (541) 344-7688
earthfirst@igc.apc.org
www.earthfirst.org
The voice of the radical environmental movement.

ECONOMIC POLICY INSTITUTE
1660 L Street NW, Suite 1200
Washington, DC 20036
(202) 775-8810
Fax: (202) 775-0819
epi@epinet.org
epinet.org

The EPI's mission is to broaden public debate over economic policy to
better serve the needs of America's
working people. The group also
seeks to expose the myths behind
the ostensible success of the neolib-
eral economic paradigm.

E.F. SCHUMACHER SOCIETY
140 Jug End Rd.
Great Barrington, MA 01230
(413) 528-1737
Fax: (413) 528-4472
efssociety@aol.com
www.smallisbeautiful.org

Promoting the ideas inherent in the
decentralist tradition celebrated by
Schumacher's 1973 classic Small is
Beautiful, this society works to
implement them through practical
programs for local economic self-
reliance.

**ELECTRONIC FRONTIER
FOUNDATION**
454 Shotwell St.
San Francisco, CA 94110
(415) 436-9333
Fax: (415) 436-9993
Eff@eff.org
www.eff.org

A leading civil liberites organization
devoted to maintaining the Internet
as a global vehicle for free speech.

**ENVIRONMENTAL NEWS
NETWORK INC.**
2020 Milvia, Suite 411
Berkeley, CA 94704
(510) 644-3661
Fax: (208) 475-7986
mgt@enn.com
www.enn.com

ENN produces news seven days a
week, with continuous updates
throughout each day posted on its
multifaceted Web site aimed at educating the public about environmental issues.

ESSENTIAL INFORMATION
P.O. Box 19405
Washington, DC 20036
(202) 387-8030
Fax: (202) 234-5176
www.essential.org

Founded in 1982 by Ralph Nader, Essential Information is a nonprofit, tax-exempt organization that provides provocative information to the public on important topics neglected by the mass media and policy makers.

FAIRNESS AND ACCURACY IN REPORTING (FAIR)
112 West 27th Street
New York, NY 10001
(212) 633-6700
Fax: (212) 727-7668
Fair@fair.org
www.fair.org

A national media watchdog group that focuses public awareness on "the narrow corporate ownership of the press," FAIR seeks to invigorate the First Amendment by advocating for greater media pluralism and the inclusion of public interest voices in national debate.

FEDERATION OF AMERICAN SCIENTISTS
1717 K Street NW, Suite 209
Washington, DC 20036
(202) 546-3300
Fax: (202) 675-1010
fas@fas.org
www.fas.org

FAS conducts analysis and critique of military science, technology and public policy.

FEMINISTS FOR FREE EXPRESSION
2525 Times Square Station
New York, NY 10108-2525
(212) 702-6292
Fax: (212) 702-6277
Freedom@well.com
www.ffeusa.org

Feminists for Free Expression is a national not-for-profit organization of feminist women and men who share a commitment both to gender equality and to preserving the individual's right to read, view, rent, or purchase media materials of their choice, free from government intervention.

FOOD & WATER INC.
389 Route 215
Walden, VT 05873
(802) 563-3300
Fax: (802) 563-3310
info@foodandwater.org
www.foodandwater.org

This organization advocates for safe
food and water, and a clean environment by educating the public on the
health and environmental dangers of
food irradiation, genetic engineering
and toxic pesticides. They are the
publishers of Wild Matters.

FOOD NOT BOMBS
P.O. Box 40485
San Francisco, CA 94140
(415) 675-9928
sffnb@tao.ca
http://sffoodnotbombs.org
An organization focused on peaceful
co-operation and hunger elimination.

**FREEDOM FORUM WORLD
CENTER**
1101 Wilson Blvd.
Arlington, VA 22209
(703) 528-0800
Fax: (703) 284-3770
News@freedomforum.org
www.freedomforum.org

A nonpartisan, international foundation dedicated to free press, free
speech and free spirit for all people.

**FREEDOM OF EXPRESSION
FOUNDATION**
171-B Claremont Ave.
Long Beach, CA 90803
(562) 985-4111
crsmith@csulb.edu
www.csulb.edu/~jvancamp/intro.html

**FREEDOM OF INFORMATION
CENTER**
University of Missouri at Columbia
133 Neff Annex, University of
Missouri-Columbia
Columbia, MO 65211-0012
(573) 882-4856
Fax: (573) 884-4963
Foi@missouri.edu
www.missouri.edu/~foiwww

Collects and indexes materials relating to controls on the flow and content of information as part of its
research on free-press issues. It also
produces an online newsletter
devoted to access.

**FREEDOM TO READ
FOUNDATION**
50 East Huron St.
Chicago, IL 60611
(800) 545-2433 x4226
Fax: (312) 280-4227
Ftrf@ala.org
www.ftrf.org

This foundation promotes and protects freedom of speech and freedom

of the press; protects the public's right to access libraries, supplies and legal counsel; and and otherwise supports libraries and librarians suffering injustices due to their defense of freedoms of speech and of the press. It is a program of the American Libraries Association.

FRIENDS OF FREE SPEECH RADIO

905 Parker Street
Berkely, CA 94710
(510) 548-0542
savepacifica@igc.org
www.savepacifica.net

Founded in April 1999, Friends works to preserve community radio stations owned by Pacifica, and to institute democratic practice in their governance.

FRIENDS OF THE EARTH

1025 Vermont Ave. NW
Washington, DC 20005
(202) 783-7400 and (877) 843-8687
Fax: (202) 783-0444
foe@foe.org
www.foe.org

Friends of the Earth is dedicated to protecting the planet from environmental degradation; committed to preserving biological, cultural, and ethnic diversity; and working to empower citizens to have an influential voice in decisions affecting the quality of their environment.

FUND FOR INVESTIGATIVE JOURNALISM

P.O. Box 60184
Washington, DC 20039-0184
(202) 362-0260
Fax: (301) 422-7449
fundfij@aol.com
www.fij.org

The Fund for Investigative Journalism awards grants to reporters working outside the protection and backing of major news organizations.

GLOBAL EXCHANGE

2017 Mission St., Suite 303
San Francisco, CA 94110
(415) 255-7296
Fax: (415) 255-7498
info@globalexchange.org
www.globalexchange.org

Global Exchange publishes books and pamphlets on various social and economic topics; promotes alternative trade for the benefit of low-income producers; helps build public awareness about human rights abuses; and sponsors Reality Tours to foreign lands, giving participants a feel for the people of a country. They remain an active participant in the "50 Years Is Enough" campaign.

GLOBALVISION

1600 Broadway, Suite 700
New York, NY 10019
(212) 246-0202
Fax: (212) 246-2677
roc@globalvision.org
www.igc.org/globalvision

An independent film and television production company specializing in an "inside-out" style of journalism, Globalvision has produced Rights & Wrongs: Human Rights Television and South Africa Now, as well as other highly acclaimed investigative documentaries.

GOVERNMENT ACCOUNTABILITY PROJECT

Mercatus Center, George Mason University,
3301 N Fairfax Dr.
Arlington, VA 22201-4433
(800) 815-5711 or (703) 993-4930
Fax: (703) 993-4935
mercatus@gmu.edu
www.governmentaccountability.org

GAP is an education, research and outreach organization that works with scholars, policy experts and government officials to bridge academic theory and real-world practice.

GRASSROOTS MEDIA NETWORK, THE

1602 Chatham
Austin, TX 78723
(512) 459-1619
rootmedia@mail.com
www.geocities.com/rootmedia/links
.html
www.crosswinds.net/~rootmedia

This media network includes the Queer News Network, Pueblos-Unidos and the Grassroots Film and Video Collective.

GREENPEACE USA

702 H Street NW
Washington, DC 20001
(800) 326-0959
Fax: (202) 462-4507
www.greenpeaceusa.org

Aiming to create a green and peaceful world, Greenpeace embraces the principle of nonviolence, rejecting attacks on people and property. It allies itself with no political party and takes no political stance.

HISPANIC EDUCATION AND MEDIA GROUP, INC.

102 Crown Circle
South San Francisco, CA 94080
(415) 331-8560
Fax: (415) 331-2636
margotsegura@aol.com
www.we-penguins.com/
  HEMG_page_1.htm

Dedicated to improving the quality of life in the Latino community, this group's main focus is on high school drop-out prevention and health issues.

HUCK BOYD NATIONAL CENTER FOR COMMUNITY MEDIA

105 Kedzie Hall, Kansas State University
Manhattan, KS 66506-1501
(785) 532-3958 and (785) 532-0721
Fax: (785) 532-5484
Huckboyd@ksu.edu
huckboyd.jmc.ksu.edu

The mission of HBNC is to strenghten local media in order to help create better, stronger communities in America.

HUMAN RIGHTS WATCH

New York Office
350 5th Avenue, 34th Floor
New York, NY 10118-3299
(212) 290-4700
Fax: (212) 736-1300
hrwnyc@hrw.org
www.hrw.org

HRW produes a variety of books and articles regarding worldwide human rights violations.

HUMAN RIGHTS WATCH

Washington DC Office
1630 Connecticut Ave. NW, Suite 500
Washington, DC 20009
(202) 612-4321
Fax: (202) 612-4333
hrwdc@hrw.org
www.hrw.org

HRW exposes and works to stop human rights abuses in over 70 countries. It struggles against summary executions, torture, restrictions on the freedoms of expression, etc.

HUMANIST MOVEMENT, THE

197 Harbord St.
Toronto, ON M5S 1H6
Canada
(416) 535-2094
roberto@ilap.com
www.cynaptica.com/hm

The Humanist Movement produces a

wide-range of media outlets at the grassroots level including neighborhood newspapers, neighborhood radio and neighborhood TV stations all over the world. These are completely non-profit, volunteer projects that focus on raising (and organizing around) issues ignored by the forces of Big Media.

INDEPENDENT PRESS ASSOCIATION

2729 Mission St., #201
San Francisco, CA 94110-3131
(415) 643-4401
Fax: (415) 643-4402
indypress@indypress.org
www.indypress.org

A membership-based association providing nuts-and-bolts technical assistance and loans, IPA networks with over 175 independent, progressive magazines and newspapers. Formed during the first Media & Democracy Congress in San Francisco (1996), the IPA promotes a diversity of voices at the newsstand.

INDEPENDENT PROGRESSIVE POLITICS NETWORK

P.O. Box 1041
Bloomfield, NJ 07003
(973) 338-5398
Fax: (973) 338-2210
indpol@igc.org
www.ippn.org

IPPN brings together organizations and individuals committed to building a united party, or alliance of parties, as a progressive alternative to the Democrats and Republicans.

INDIGENOUS SUPPORT COALITION OF OREGON

Big Mountain
P.O. Box 11715
Eugene, OR 97440
(541) 683-2789
isco@efn.org, bigmnt@efn.org,
lpsg@efn.org
www.hri.ca/partners/naps/Organizat
ions/viewit.cfm?ID=6

Information about and support for Native American issues in the Northwest.

INFACT: CAMPAIGN FOR CORPORATE ACCOUNTABILITY

46 Plympton St.
Boston, MA 02118
(617) 695-2525
Fax: (617) 695-2626
info@infact.org
www.infact.org

Infact is a national grassroots corporate watchdog organization. Founded in 1977, Infact is best known for its successful Nestle and GE boycott campaigns, and its new film Making a Killing.

INSTITUTE FOR FOOD AND DEVELOPMENT POLICY

398 60th Street
Oakland, CA 94618
(510) 654-4400
Fax: (510) 654-4551
foodfirst@foodfirst.org
www.foodfirst.org

This group works to mobilize and organize people around the world to support the struggles of the hungry for the right to feed themselves. They promote awareness of economic, social and cultural human rights and publish the Food First News.

INSTITUTE FOR LOCAL SELF-RELIANCE

2425 18th Street NW (National Office)
Washington, DC 20009-2096
(202) 232-4108
Fax: (202) 332-0463
info@ilsr.org
www.ilsr.org

This 27-year-old nonprofit research and educational organization provides technical assistance and information on environmentally sound economic development strategies. They are publishers of the Home Town Advantage E-Bulletin.

INSTITUTE FOR MEDIA POLICY AND CIVIL SOCIETY

207 W Hastings St., Suite 910
Vancouver, BC V6B 1H7
Canada
(604) 682-1953 and (877) 232-0122
Fax: (604) 682-4353
media@impacs.org
www.impacs.bc.ca

The group's mission is to build strong communities by training and educating Canadian civil society organizations.

INSTITUTE FOR PUBLIC ACCURACY

65 9th Street, Suite 3
San Francisco, CA 94103
(415) 552-5378
Fax: (415) 552-6787
institute@igc.org
www.accuracy.org/

The Institute serves as a nationwide consortium of progressive policy researchers, scholars and activists, providing the media with timely information and perspectives on a wide range of issues.

INSTITUTE FOR SOUTHERN STUDIES, THE

P.O. Box 531
Durham, NC 27702-0531
(919) 419-8311
Fax: (919) 419-8315
info@i4south.org
www.southernstudies.org

The only region-wide organization combining the in-depth investigations essential to understanding the South with the grassroots organizing needed to change it.

INSTITUTE OF GLOBAL COMMUNICATIONS

(Formerly the Institute For Policy Studies)
P.O. Box 29904
San Francisco, CA 94129
(202) 234-9382
Fax: (202) 387-7915
support@igc.apc.org
www.igc.org/igc/gateway/index.html

Since 1963 IPS has been the nation's leading center of progressive research linked to activism.

INTERACTION

1717 Massachusetts Ave. NW, Suite 701
Washington, DC 20036
(202) 667-8227
Fax: (202) 667-8236
ia@interaction.org
www.interaction.org

A coalition of over 150 U.S.-based nonprofits working to promote human dignity and development in 165 countries, Interaction is active in programs to ease human suffering and to strengthen people's ability to help themselves.

INTERHEMISPHERIC RESOURCE CENTER (IRC)

P.O. Box 4506
Albuquerque, NM 87196-4506
(505) 842-8288
Fax: (505) 246-1601
resourcectr@igc.apc.org
www.irc-online.org

IRC believes that U.S. foreign policy and international economic relations should be reshaped to support a global economy that fosters broad development for all nations, participatory political systems and environmentally sustainable economic growth.

INTERNATIONAL ACTION CENTER

39 West 14th Street, # 206
New York, NY 10011
(212) 633-6646
Fax: (212) 633-2889
iacenter@action-mail.org
www.iacenter.org

Initiated in 1992 by former Attorney General Ramsey Clark and other anti-war activists, IAC coordinates international meetings, teach-ins, massive demonstrations, publishes news releases and produces video documentaries.

INTERNATIONAL CONSORTIUM OF INVESTIGATIVE JOURNALISTS (ICIJ)

Center for Public Integrity
910 17th Street NW, 7th Floor
Washington, DC 20006
(202) 466-1300
Fax: (202) 466-1101
info@icij.org
www.icij.org

ICIJ is a working consortium of leading investigative reporters from around the world that sponsors investigations into pressing issues that transcend national borders.

INTERNATIONAL FORUM ON GLOBALIZATION

The Thoreau Center for Sustainability
1009 General Kennedy Ave., #2
San Francisco, CA 94129
(415) 561-7650
Fax: (415) 561-7651
ifg@ifg.org
www.ifg.org

An alliance of sixty leading activists, scholars, economists, researchers and writers, the IFG provides analysis, joint activity and public education in response to economic globalization.

INTERNATIONAL MEDIA PROJECT

National Radio Project
1714 Franklin, #311
Oakland, CA 94612
(510) 251-1332
Fax: (510) 251-1342
laura@radioproject.org
www.radioproject.org

The International Media Project, aiming to air the voices of those silenced by the mass media, produces a half-hour, weekly public affairs radio program called "Making Contact." Making Contact is heard on 150 stations nationally, in Canada and South Africa, and is broadcast on the Internet as "Radio for Peace International."

INVESTIGATIVE JOURNALISM PROJECT

Fund for Constitutional Government (FCG)
122 Maryland Ave. NE, Suite 300
Washington, DC 20002
(202) 546-3732
Fax: (202) 543-3156
www.epic.org/fcg/projects.html

The Investigative Journalism Project is an ongoing vehicle through which FCG provides financing and encouragement to journalists committed to uncovering stories of corruption in government and violations of constitutional principles.

IRE (INVESTIGATIVE REPORTERS AND EDITORS, INC.)

Missouri School of Journalism,
138 Neff Annex
Columbia, MO 65211
(573) 882-2042
Fax: (573) 882-5431
info@ire.org
www.ire.org

Investigative Reporters and Editors, Inc. is a grassroots nonprofit organization dedicated to improving the quality of investigative reporting within the field of journalism.

JUST THINK FOUNDATION

29 Mesa St., Suite 106 Presidio Park
San Francisco, CA 94129
(415) 561-2900
Fax: (415) 561-2901
think@justthink.org
www.justthink.org

The Just Think Foundation (JTF) is a dynamic nonprofit dedicated to offering young people literacy education and providing them with the skills to be critical thinkers and creative producers. Just Think develops curriculum and has delivered media

literacy education programs in schools and online.

KLANWATCH AND MILITIA TASKFORCE

Southern Poverty Law Center
400 Washington Ave.
Montgomery, AL 36104
(334) 264-0286
Fax: (334) 264-8891
www.splcenter.org/splc.html

In 1981, in the wake an upsurge of KKK violence, the Southern Poverty Law Center created a new department, Klanwatch. Monitoring organized hate activity across the country, Klanwatch was developed as one of the center's many strategies to hold white supremacist leaders accountable for violence committed by their followers.

LIVELIHOOD

1611 Telegraph Ave., Suite 1550
Oakland, CA 94612
(510) 268-9675
Fax: (510) 268-3606
info@theworkinggroup.org
www.pbs.org/livelihood or
www.pbs.org/noit

A nonprofit media production company focused on ordinary, hardworking Americans, Livelihood has produced the "We Do The Work" series and the "Not In Our Town" specials, which gained national recognition for showcasing positive community response to and intolerance of hate violence.

LOOMPANICS UNLIMITED

P.O. Box 1197
Port Townsend, WA 98368
(360) 385-2230
Fax: (360) 385-7785
operations@loompanics.com
www.loompanics.com

Champions of the First Amendment, LU publishes and distributes publications covering a variety of controversial, unusual and underground topics. Their complete catalogue is available online.

LOS ANGELES CALIFA, INC.

P.O. Box 8181
Los Angeles, CA 90008-8181
(323) 751-1353
Fax: (323) 930-2243
califa_inc@hotmail.com
www.100net.com/calif

This group believes that a more informed, concerned and participatory citizenry, recognizing and acknowledging the diverse ethnicities of which Los Angeles is composed, can work together and in concert with civic leaders to rebuild a solid and stable Los Angeles.

MACROMEDIA

Corporate Headquarters
600 Townsend St.
San Francisco, CA 94103
(415) 252-2000
Fax: (415) 626-0554
www.mosaictv.com

Macromedia provides the global truth perspective for black people, featuring video lectures, research and newscoverage that is ignored or deliberately hidden by mainstream media.

MEDIA ALLIANCE

814 Mission St., Suite 205
San Francisco, CA 94103
(415) 546-6334
Fax: (415) 546-6218
info@media-alliance.org
www.media-alliance.org

These publishers of *Mediafile* provide review and analysis of San Francisco Bay area media issues. MA supports progressive journalists to ensure a broad range of viewpoints in the media; holds corporate media outlets accountable to local communities' needs; and trains people under-represented in media to tell their own stories.

MEDIA COALITION/AMERICANS FOR CONSTITUTIONAL FREEDOM

139 Fulton St., Suite 302
New York, NY 10038
(212) 587-4025
Fax: (212) 587-2436
mediacoalition@mediacoalition.org
www.mediacoalition.org

This organization defends the American public's First Amendment right of access to the broadest possible range of opinion and entertainment.

MEDIA EDUCATION FOUNDATION, THE

26 Center St.
Northampton, MA 01060
(800) 897-0089 and (413) 584-8500
Fax: (800) 659-6882 or (413) 586-8398
info@mediaed.org
www.mediaed.org

MEF provides media research and production fostering analytical media literacy. It has produced and distributed a number of educational videos including *The Myth of the Liberal Media* (with Noam Chomsky and Ed Herman), *Killing Us Softly III* (with Jean Kilbourne) and *Tough Guise: Violence, Media & the Crisis of Masculinity* (with Jackson Katz).

MEDIA ISLAND INTERNATIONAL

P.O.Box 7204
Olympia, WA 98507
(360) 352-8526
Fax: (360) 352-8490
mii@olywa.net
www.mediaisland.org

MII works to popularize sociopolitical justice and environmental frontline issues by linking issue-focused organizations with media organizations and mapping international allies for change.

MEDIACHANNEL

MediaChannel is a nonprofit, public interest organization dedicated to global media issues. MediaChannel offers news, reports and commentary from our international network of media-issues organizations and publications, as well as original features from contributors and staff.

MEDIAVISION

P.O. Box 1045
Boston, MA 02130
(617) 522-2923
Fax: (617) 522-1872
mediavi@aol.com

Working for wider exposure of progressive views through mass media, MediaVision provides strategic media consulting, training and other services for organizations and individuals.

MINUTEMAN MEDIA

32 Allen Rd.
Norwalk, CT 06851
(203) 846-1109
Fax: (203) 846-1109
speed1212@aol.com
www.tidescenter.org/project_detail.c
fm?id=170.0

Minuteman Media's goal is to present regular, free, high-quality competing newspaper columns to small newspapers throughout the country in an effort to counteract the onslaught of right-wing editorials and op-ed pieces.

NATIONAL ASIAN AMERICAN TELECOMMUNICATIONS ASSOCIATION

346 Ninth Street, 2nd floor
San Francisco, CA 94103
(415) 863-0814
Fax: (415) 863-7428
naata@naatanet.org
www.naatanet.org

This organization seeks to increase Asian and Pacific Islander participation in the media and promote fair and accurate coverage of these communities.

NATIONAL ASSOCIATION OF BLACK JOURNALISTS

University of Maryland
8701-A Adelphi Rd.
Adelphi, MD 20783-1716
(301) 445-7100
Fax: (301) 445-7101
nabj@nabj.org
www.nabj.org

NABJ's mission is to strengthen ties among African-American journalists, promote diversity in newsrooms, and expand job opportunities and recruiting activities for established African-American journalists and students.

NATIONAL ASSOCIATION OF HISPANIC JOURNALISTS

1000 National Press Building
Washington, DC 20045-2001
(888) 346-NAHJ and (202) 662-7145
Fax: (202) 662-7144
nahj@nahj.org
www.nahj.org

NAHJ is dedicated to the recognition and professional advancement of Hispanics in the news industry.

NATIONAL ASSOCIATION OF MINORITY MEDIA EXECUTIVES

1921 Gallows Rd. Suite 600
Vienna, VA 22182
(703) 893-2410 and (888) 968-7658
Fax: (703) 893-2414
www.namme.org

NATIONAL ASSOCIATION OF RADIO TALK SHOW HOSTS
2791 S Buffalo Dr.
Las Vegas, NV 89117
(702) 248-4884
Fax: (702) 889-1474
carolnashe@mindspring.com
carol@talkshowhosts.com
www.talkshowhosts.com

This trade association for the radio talk industry provides a resource guide to talk radio worldwide.

NATIONAL CENTER ON DISABILITY AND JOURNALISM
944 Market St., Suite 829
San Francisco, CA 94102
(415) 291-0868
Fax: (415) 291-0869
ncdj@ncdj.org
www.ncdj.org

NCDJ is a new nonprofit organization whose mission is to improve the fairness, accuracy and diversity of news reporting on disability by developing tools to help journalists and educators examine the complexity of disability issues from differing perspectives.

NATIONAL COALITION AGAINST CENSORSHIP
275 7th Avenue
New York, NY 10001
(212) 807-6222
Fax: (212) 807-6245
ncac@ncac.org
www.ncac.org

Founded in 1974, NCAC is an alliance of over 50 national nonprofit organizations. It works to educate members and the public at large about the dangers of censorship and how to oppose it.

NATIONAL COALITION TO PROTECT POLITICAL FREEDOM (NCPPF)
Interreligious Foundation for Community Organization (IFCO)
3321-12th Street NE
Washington, DC 20017
(202) 529-4225
Fax: (202) 526-4611
ifco@igc.apc.org
www.ifconews.org/ncppf.html

A national membership organization dedicated to protecting the First Amendment and due process rights of all Americans, the NCPPF defends the right of people to give humanitarian and political support to causes in the U.S. and abroad. It connects individuals under attack with lawyers working on these issues and provides legal support and briefs to educate individuals on strategic media communication.

NATIONAL COMMITTEE AGAINST REPRESSIVE LEGISLATION (NCARL)

3321 12th Street NE
Washington, DC 20017
(202) 529-4225
Fax: (202) 526-4611
ncarl@aol.com

NCARL focuses on reducing repressive legislation.

NATIONAL CONFERENCE OF EDITORIAL WRITERS (NCEW)

6223 Executive Blvd.
Rockville, MD 20852
(301) 984-3015
Fax: (301) 231-0026
ncewhqs@erols.com
www.ncew.org

Since 1946 NCEW has been dedicated to stimulating the conscience and quality of the editorial.

NATIONAL LABOR COMMITTEE

275 7th Avenue, 15th Floor
New York, NY 10001
(212) 242-3002
Fax: (212) 242-3821
nlc@nlcnet.org
www.nlcnet.org

Working to educate and actively engage the U.S. public and media on human and labor rights abuses by corporations, the NLC through this education and activism aims to end labor and human rights violations, ensure a living wage and help workers and their families live and work with dignity.

NATIONAL LESBIAN AND GAY JOURNALISTS ASSOCIATION, THE (NLGJA)

1420 K Street NW,Suite 910
Washington, DC 20005
(202) 588-9888
Fax: (202) 588-1818
info@nlgja.org
www.nlgja.org

NLGJA works from within the news industry to foster fair and accurate coverage of lesbian and gay issues and oppose newroom bias against lesbians, gay men and all other minorities.

NATIONAL RADIO PROJECT

1916 Telegraph Ave.
Oakland, CA 94612
(510) 251-1332
Fax: (510) 251-1342
www.radioproject.org

The National Radio Project (NRP) is an independent nonprofit media organization founded in 1994. NRP heightens public consciousness, broadens debate on critical social issues and encourages civic participation by giving voice to diverse perspectives and opinions not typically heard in the mass media.

NATIONAL TELEMEDIA COUNCIL
120 E Wilson St.
Madison, WI 53703
(608) 257-7712
Fax: (608) 257-7714
ntc@danenet.wicip.org
danenet.wicip.org/ntc

Publishers of *Telemedium: The Journal of Media Literacy*, NTC is a national nonprofit educational organization that promotes media literacy education with a positive, nonjudgmental philosophy. The oldest national media literacy organization in the U.S., it is in its 49th year.

NATIONAL WOMEN'S HEALTH NETWORK
514 10th Street NW, Suite 400
Washington, DC 20004
(202) 347-1140 and (202) 628-7814
Fax: (202) 347-1168
www.womenshealthnetwork.org

This network, focusing on women's health and related issues, is the only national public-interest membership organization dedicated exclusively to women's health. NWHN publishes a bimonthly newsletter for members entitled *Network News.*

NATIONAL WRITERS UNION (EAST)
National office, East
113 University Place, 6th floor
New York, NY 10003
(212) 254-0279
Fax: (212) 254-0673
nwu@nwu.org
www.nwu.org

Publishers of *American Writer*, a national quarterly.

NATIONAL WRITERS UNION (WEST)
337 17th Street, #101
Oakland, CA 94612
(510) 839-0110
Fax: (510) 839-6097
nwu@nwu.org
www.nwu.org

NET ACTION
601 Van Ness Ave., #631
San Francisco, CA 94102
(415) 775-8674
Fax: (415) 673-3813
audrie@netaction.org
www.netaction.org

NA educates the public, policy-makers and media about technology policy issues; trains Internet users to use technology for organizing, outreach, and advocacy; and promotes universal accessibility and affordability of information technology.

NEW DAY FILMS

22-D Hollywood Ave.
Hohokus, NJ 07423
(201) 652-6590
Fax: (201) 652-1973
pgoudvis@mindspring.com
heidi@spiritproductions.org
www.newday.com

New Day Films is a film/video distribution co-operative. Its films focus on multiculturalism and diversity; physical and mental health; social and political history; global and community politics; media, art and culture; gender and socialization; and young adult and family issues.

NEW MEXICO MEDIA LITERACY PROJECT

6400 Wyoming Blvd. NE
Albuquerque, NM 87109
(505) 828-3129
Fax: (505) 828-3320
mccannon@aa.edu or scottd@aa.edu
Torres@aa.edu
www.nmmlp.org

A regional media education organization in the U.S.

NEW YORK FOUNDATION FOR THE ARTS

155 Avenue of the Americas, 14th Floor
New York, NY 10013-1507
(212) 366-6900
Fax: (212) 366-1778
nyfaweb@nyfa.org
www.artswire.org

The NCFE is an educational and advocacy network of artists, arts organizations, audience members and concerned citizens formed to protect and extend freedom of artistic expression and fight censorship throughout the United States.

NEWSWATCH

Marnard Institute for Journalism Education
409 13th Street, 9th Floor
Oakland, CA 94612
(510) 839-2807
Fax: (415) 338-2084
newsproj@mindspring.com
newswatch.sfsu.edu

A media watch organization and freedom of information advocacy group.

NEWSWATCH CANADA

School of Communication, Simon
Fraser University
8888 University Dr.
Burnaby, BC V5A 1S6
Canada
(604) 291-4905
Fax: (604) 291-3687
newswtch@sfu.ca
newswatch.cprost.sfu.ca

A Canadian media watch organization and freedom of information advocacy group.

NICAR: NATIONAL INSTITUTE FOR COMPUTER-ASSISTED REPORTING

Missouri School of Journalism
138 Neff Annex
Columbia, MO 65211
(573) 882-2042 or 3364
Fax: (573) 882-5431 and (573) 884-5549
info@ire.org
www.nicar.org

A program of Investigative Reporters and Editors, Inc. and the Missouri School of Journalism, NICAR was founded in 1989. Since that time it has trained thousands of journalists in the practical skills of finding, prying loose and analyzing electronic information.

OCTOBER 22 COALITION TO STOP POLICE BRUTALITY

P.O. Box 2627
New York, NY 10009
(888) NoBrutality and (212) 477-8062
Fax: (212) 477-8015
office@october22.org
www.office@october22.org

This coalition works to build toward a national day of protest, on October 22nd, to stop police brutality, repression and the criminalization of a generation. Those most targeted stand together with clergy, lawyers, artists, prominent people and others to shout in a unified voice: NO MORE POLICE BRUTALITY! The Coalition, along with the Anthony Baez Foundation and the National Lawyers Guild, is a member of the The Stolen Lives Project, which collects and documents the names of victims killed by law enforcement agencies since 1990.

OFFLINE
Offline West
P.O. Box 45517
Seattle, WA 98145-0517
(206) 789-3597
info@offlinenetworks.org
www.offlinenetworks.org

A national arts organization that screens cable television and distributes independently produced films and videos,Offline serves as a creative conduit for numerous national and international screenings, arts organizations, micro-cinemas, festivals, netcast providers and artists.

PACIFIC NEWS SERVICE
660 Market St., Room 210
San Francisco, CA 94104
(415) 438-4755
Fax: (415) 438-4935
pacificnews@pacificnews.org
www.pacificnews.org

These publishers of *The Beat Within*, *Yo!* and *New California* produce an article per day for reprint in a variety of newspapers worldwide.

PAPER TIGER TELEVISION
339 Lafayette St.
New York, NY 10012
(212) 420-9045
Fax: (212) 420-8223
info@papertiger.org
www.papertiger.org

A nonprofit volunteer collective that has been pioneering media criticism through video since 1981, Paper Tiger Television conducts workshops, creates installations and produces videos. Its programs address issues of democratic communication, media representation and the economics of the information industry It smashes the myths of the information industry. Video activism + love = Paper Tiger.

PARADIGM NEW MEDIA GROUP
1307 Washington Ave., Suite 400
St. Louis, MO 63103
(314) 436-4003
Fax: (314) 436-0224
info@pnmg.com
www.pnmg.com

A private network promoting individual, community and/or planetary evolution via print, Internet, radio, TV, music, theater, etc.

PAUL ROBESON FUND FOR INDEPENDENT MEDIA, THE
666 Broadway, Suite 500
New York, NY 10012
(212) 529-5300 x307
Fax: (212) 982-9272
trinh.duong@fex.org
www.namac.org/Directory/org_data/prfd.html

The PR Fund supports media

activism and grassroots organizing by local, state, national and international organizations and individual media producers by funding radio, film and video productions. It publishes a newsletter called *Funding Exchange.*

PEACE ACTION
1819 H Street NW, Suite 420 and 425
Washington, DC 20006
(202) 862-9740
Fax: (202) 862-9762
slynch@peace-action.org
www.webcom.com/peaceact

The largest membership and activist network of any peace and justice organization in the country, Peace Action works for policy changes at municipal, state, national and international levels.

PEOPLE AGAINST RACIST TERROR (PART)
P.O. Box 1055
Culver City, CA 90232-1055
(310) 495-0299
part2001@usa.net
www.antiracist.org/issues.html

A grassroots organization focusing on anti-racist activism, research and education,PART is committed to ending colonialism, sexism and all forms of oppression and exploitation.They are the publishers of *Turning the Tide.*

PEOPLES VIDEO NETWORK
International Action Center
39 West 14th Street, #206
New York, NY 10011
(212) 633-6646
Fax: (212) 633-2889
pvnnyc@peoplesvideo.org
www.peoplesvideo.org

This group of video activists is committed to publicizing stories of the struggles of poor and oppressed people that the corporate media will not cover. It reaches 50 cities every week and has many special editions.

PEW OCEANS COMMISSION
2101 Wilson Blvd., Suite 550
Arlington, VA 22201
(703) 516-0624
Fax: (703) 516-9551
www.pewoceans.org

The Pew Oceans Commission is an independent group of American leaders conducting a national dialogue on the policies needed to restore and protect living marine resources in U.S. waters.

PIRATE TELEVISION
KCAT Channel 20
c/o X-TV Pirate Television
16433 Wedgeworth Dr.
Hacienda Heights, CA 91745
(626) 333-2427
crumyshon@aol.com
www.geocities.com/thing73vw2002/
X-TV2.htm

PT produces a weekly public access
program called "Crack the CIA."

**POLITICAL RESEARCH
ASSOCIATES (PRA)**
1310 Broadway, Suite 201
Somerville, MA 02144-1731
(617) 666-5300
Fax: (617) 666-6622
pra@igc.org
www.publiceye.org

PRA focuses on research and analysis of right wing political groups and
their influence over media and policy making.

PROGRESSIVE CAUCUS
U.S. House of Representatives
213 Cannon House Office Building
Washington, DC 20515-4501
(202) 225-4115
Fax: (202) 225-6790
david.sirota@mail.house.gov
www.bernie.house.gov/pc

"The members of the Progressive
Caucus share a common belief in
the principles of social and economic justice, nondiscrimination, and
tolerance in America and in our
relationships with other countries."—Lynn Woolsey

PROGRESSIVE MEDIA PROJECT
409 E Main St.
Madison, WI 53703
(608) 257-4626
Fax: (608) 257-3373
pmproj@progressive.org
www.progressive.org

This project provides opinion pieces
from a progressive perspective to
daily and weekly newspapers all
over the country.

PROJECT CENSORED
Sociology Department, Sonoma
State University
1801 E. Cotati Ave.
Rohnert Park, CA 94928-3609
(707) 664-2500
Fax: (707) 664-2108
censored@sonoma.edu
www.projectcensored.org

A faculty/student media research
project dedicated to building free
democratic news systems, Project
Censored produces an annual year-
book that discusses the year's top 25
under-reported stories.

PROJECT ON GOVERNMENT OVERSIGHT

666 11th Street NW, Suite 500
Washington, DC 20001
(202) 347-1122
Fax: (202) 347-1116
pogo@pogo.org or defense@pogo.org
www.pogo.org

The goal of POGO is to investigate, expose and remedy abuses of power, mismanagement and subservience to special interests by the federal government.

PUBLIC CAMPAIGN

1320 19th Street NW, Suite M-1
Washington, DC 20036
(202) 293-0222
Fax: (202) 293-0202
info@publicampaign.org
www.publicampaign.org

A nonprofit, nonpartisan organization dedicated to sweeping reforms to dramatically reduce the role of special interest money in America's elections and the influence of big contributors in American politics.

PUBLIC CITIZEN

Global Trade Watch
1600 20th Street NW
Washington, DC 20009
(202)588-1000
www.citizen.org

Public Citizen is a national, non-profit consumer advocacy organization founded by Ralph Nader in 1971 to represent consumer interests in Congress, the executive branch and the courts. We fight for openness and democratic accountability in government; for the right of consumers to seek redress in the courts; for clean, safe and sustainable energy sources; for social and economic justice in trade policies; for strong health, safety and environmental protections; and for safe, effective and affordable prescription drugs and health care.

PUBLIC MEDIA CENTER

466 Green St.
San Francisco, CA 94133
(415) 434-1403
Fax: (415) 986-6779
info@publicmediacenter.org
www.publicmediacenter.org

A nonprofit, public interest advertising agency focused on social, political and environmental issues.

REAL NEWS NETWORK
276 King St. W
Kitchener, ON
Canada
(519) 893-5321
Fax: (519) 893-0735
pboini@realnewsnetwork.com
www.realnewsnetwork.com

"Providing vital human information," RNN publishes public interest journalism and *Real Society: Canada's Real News Magazine*.

REDEFINING PROGRESS
1904 Franklin St., 6th Floor
Oakland, CA 94612
(510) 444-3041
Fax: (510) 444-3191
info@rprogress.org
www.rprogress.org

Redefining Progress is a nonprofit public policy and research organization that develops policies and tools to reorient the economy so it will value people and nature first.

REPORTER'S COMMITTEE FOR FREEDOM OF THE PRESS
1815 N Fort Myer Dr., Suite 900
Arlington, VA 22209
(800) 336-4243 and (703) 807-2100
Fax: (703) 807-2109
rcfp@rcfp.org
www.rcfp.org

This publisher of *News Media Update* and *News Media and The Law* serves as a major national and international resource in free speech issues, disseminating information in a variety of forms: including a quarterly legal review, a biweekly newsletter, a 24-hour hotline and various handbooks on media law issues.

SEATTLE INDEPENDENT FILM AND VIDEO CONSORTIUM
2318 2nd Avenue, PMB #313-A
Seattle, WA 98121
(206) 568-6051
info@blackchair.com
www.blackchair.com/ix/index-2.htm

This consortium furthers press and public awareness of independent media-makers. It increases dialogue between regional, national and international organizations via micro-cinema screenings, television, netcasting, salon activity and art events.

SOCIETY OF ENVIRONMENTAL JOURNALISTS
P.O. Box 2492
Jenkintown, PA 19046
(215) 884-8174
Fax: (215) 884-8175
sej@sej.org
www.sej.org

SEJ is dedicated to supporting environmental journalists and furthering environmental journalism, including in their own SEJournal.

SOCIETY OF PROFESSIONAL JOURNALISTS
3909 N Meridian St.
Indianapolis, IN 46208
(317) 927-8000
Fax: (317) 920-4789
questions@spj.org
www.spj.org

SPJ is the nation's largest and most broad-based journalism organization. It is a not-for-profit organization made up of 13,500 members dedicated to encouraging the free practice of journalism, stimulating high standards of ethical behavior and perpetuating a free press: that is, "Improving & Protecting Journalism."

SOUTHWEST ALTERNATE MEDIA PROJECT
1519 W Main St.
Houston, TX 77006
(713) 522-8592
Fax: (713) 522-0953
info@swamp.org
www.swamp.org

A nonprofit media center promoting the creation and appreciation of film and video as art forms suited for a multicultural public.

SOUTHWEST RESEARCH AND INFORMATION CENTER
P.O. Box 4524
Albuquerque, NM 87106
(505) 262-1862
Fax: (505) 262-1864
Admin@sric.org
www.sric.org

Southwest Research and Information Center (SRIC) exists to provide timely, accurate information to the public on matters that affect the environment, human health and communities in order to protect natural resources, promote citizen participation and ensure environmental and social justice now and for future generations. SRIC's publication is the *Workbook*.

STRATEGY CENTER PUBLICATIONS
3780 Wilshire Blvd., Suite 1200
Los Angeles, CA 90010
(213) 387-2800
Fax: (213) 387-3500
laborctr@igc.org
www.thestrategycenter.org

Strategy Center Publications publishes and distributes many books, working papers and article reprints, as well as the audiotapes and videos of the Labor/Community Strategy Center.

TELEVISION PROJECT, THE
2311 Kimball Place
Silver Springs, MD 20910
(301) 588-4001
Fax: (301) 588-4001
info@tvp.org
www.tvp.org

This organization helps parents understand how television affects their families and community, and proposes alternatives that foster positive emotional, cognitive and spiritual development within families and communities.

THOMAS JEFFERSON CENTER FOR THE PROTECTION OF FREE EXPRESSION, THE
400 Peter Jefferson Place
Charlottesville, VA 22911-8691
(434) 295-4789
Fax: (434) 296-3621
freespch@tjcenter.org
www.tjcenter.org

An organization devoted to the defense of free expression in all its forms.

THIRD WORLD NETWORK
228 Macalister Rd.
Penang, Malaysia
+60(4)226-6728/226-6159
Fax: +60(4)226-4505
twn.features@conf.igc.apc
twin.info@conf.igc.apc
www.twnside.org.sg

Publishers of *Third World Resurgence*, this international network of groups and individuals is involved in efforts to bring about a greater articulation of the needs and rights of people in the Third World; a fair distribution of world resources; and ecologically sustainable forms of development to fulfill human needs.

THIRD WORLD NEWSREEL
545 8th Avenue, 10th Floor
New York, NY 10018
(212) 947-9277
Fax: (212) 594-6417
twn@twn.org
www.twn.org

Founded in 1967, Third World Newsreel is one of the oldest alternative media arts organizations in the United States. We are committed to the creation and appreciation of independent and social issue media by and about people of color, and the peoples of developing countries, around the world.

TORONTO VIDEO ACTIVIST COLLECTIVE
Toronto, ON
Canada
hermolin@pathcom.com
tvac@tao.ca
www.tvac.ca

Focused on documenting and promoting social and environmental justice movements, TVAC tapes events, organizes screenings and conducts workshops on video activism.

TRANSITIONSMEDIA

2 Monte Alto Court
Santa Fe, NM 87505
(505) 466-2616
Fax: (505) 466-2617
host@transradio.com
www.transradio.com

Producers of the weekly global netcast and FM broadcast "Transitions Radio Magazine," TransitionsMedia addresses social issues, focusing on topics not covered accurately or fairly by the mainstream media. TransitionsMedia also produces multimedia events, video interviews and video products on the above topics.

UNITY

1601 N Kent St., Suite 1003
Arlington, VA 22209
(703) 469-2100
Fax: (703) 469-2108
info@unityjournalists.org
www.unityjournalists.org

Unity is in strategic alliance with several cultural journalist organizations including AAJA, NABJ, NAHJ and NAJA.

UPPNET: UNION PRODUCERS AND PROGRAMMERS NETWORK

c/o Labor Education Service Union
Producers and Programmers
Network
437 Magt & Econ Building
271 19th Avenue South.
University of Minnesota
Minneapolis, MN 55455
(612) 624-4326
uppnet@labornet.org
www.mtn.org/jsee/uppnet.html

UPPNET is organized to promote the production and use of TV and radio shows pertinent to the cause of organized labor and working people.

VANGUARD COMMUNICATIONS

2121 K Street NW, Suite 300
Washington, DC 20037
(202) 331-4323
Fax: (202) 331-9420
www.vancomm.com

A full-service strategic communications company that develops and implements advocacy communications campaigns on critical environmental, health and social justice issues, Vanguard also conducts media training, produces award-winning publications, and stages national and local media events. In addition, it has created innovative partnerships between many diverse organizations.

WE INTERRUPT THIS MESSAGE

160 14th Street
San Francisco, CA 94103
(415) 621-3302
Fax: (415) 621-3319
interrupt@igc.org
www.interrupt.org/witm.html

We Interrupt This Message builds capacity in public interest groups to do traditional media and publicity work, as well as to reframe public debate and interrupt media stereotypes.

WHISPERED MEDIA

P.O. Box 40130
San Francisco, CA 94140
(415) 789-8484
info@videoactivism.org
www.videoactivism.org

This group provides video witnessing, video post-production and media resources for grassroots activist groups. It facilitates the Bay Area Video Activist Network (VAN) and specializes in direct action campaigns.

WOMEN FOR MUTUAL SECURITY

Women's Peace Movement and MEDIA Woman's International Network
1 Romilias St., 146 71 Kastri
Athens, Greece
+30(1)623-0830
Fax: +30(1)801-2850
mpap.ath.forthnet.gr@forthnet.gr
web.tiscali.it/WIN/008.html

WMS is a network of women's organizations and individuals committed to making a paradigm shift in the world from a hierarchical and violent mode of society to a new cooperative and peaceful model. WMS manages the Progressive International Media Exchange.

WOMEN'S INSTITUTE FOR FREEDOM OF THE PRESS

1940 Calvert St.
Washington, DC 20009-1502
(202) 265-6707
Fax: (202) 986-6355
allen@wifp.org
www.wifp.org

This institute explores ways to assure that everyone has equal access to publicly speak for themselves.

WORLD PRESS FREEDOM COMMITTEE
11690-C Sunrise Valley Dr.
Reston, VA 20191
(703) 715-9811
Fax: (703) 620-6790
freepress@wpfc.org
www.wpfc.org

A coordination group of national and international news media organizations, WPFC is an umbrella organization that includes 44 journalistic organizations united in the defense and promotion of freedom.

WORLD RESOURCES INSTITUTE
10 G Street NE , Suite 800
Washington, DC 20002
(202) 729-7600
Fax: (202) 729-7610
front@wri.org
www.wri.org

WRI is an environmental think tank that goes beyond research to find practical ways to protect the earth and improve people's lives, and to catalyze public and private action.

WORLDWATCH INSTITUTE
1776 Massachusetts Ave. NW
Washington, DC 20036-1904
(202) 452-1999
Fax: (202) 296-7365
worldwatch@worldwatch.org
www.worldwatch.org

The Worldwatch Institute is dedicated to fostering the evolution of an environmentally sustainable society. The Institute seeks to achieve this goal through research and investigative journalisms. Worldwatch provides an online global environmental media center.

YOUTH MEDIA COUNCIL
1611 Telegraph Ave.,Suite 510
Oakland, CA 94612
(510) 444-0640
info@youthmediacouncil.org
www.youthmediacouncil.org

Eight youth organizations in the San Francisco Bay area have partnered with We Interrupt This Message and the Movement Strategy Center to launch an organizing, youth development, media strategy, media watchdog project.

ABILITIES
489 College St., Suite 501
Toronto, ON M6G 1A5
Canada
(416) 923-1885
Fax: (416) 923-9829
info@enablelink.org
www.abilities.ca

Published by the Canadian Abilities Foundation, this lifestyle magazine is for people with disabilities; their families and friends; and professionals in the field.

ABORIGINAL VOICES
116 Spadina Ave., Suite 201
Toronto, ON M5V 2K6
Canada
(800) 324-6067 and (416) 703-4577
Fax: (416) 703-4581
info@aboriginalvoices.com
www.cmpa.ca/si2.html

A magazine focusing on indigenous art, literature, culture, media and entertainment.

ABOUT...TIME MAGAZINE
283 Genesee St.
Rochester, NY 14611-3496
(716) 235-7150
fax: (716) 235-7195

atmag@abouttimemag.com
www.abouttimemag.com

This monthly magazine focuses on issues of international, national and regional importance reflecting the African-American experience.

ADBUSTERS: A MAGAZINE OF MEDIA AND ENVIRONMENTAL STRATEGIES
1243 West 7th Avenue
Vancouver, BC V6H 1B7
(604) 736-9401 and (800) 663-1243
Fax: (604) 737-6021
adbusters@adbusters.org
www.adbusters.org

This journal of the Media Foundation provides strategies for fighting commercialism and advertising.

ADVOCATE
P.O. Box 4371
Los Angeles, CA 90078
Fax: (323) 467-0173 Editorial Fax: (323) 467-6805
newsroom@advocate.com
www.advocate.com

A leading national gay and lesbian news magazine.

AFRICAN-AMERICAN OBSERVER

303 West 42nd Street, Suite 515
New York, NY 10036
(212) 586-4141
Fax: (212) 586-4272
blacknewswatch@aol.com

A weekly newspaper on African-American issues; publishers of the *Daily Journal*.

AFSCME LEADER (PUBLIC EMPLOYEE)

1625 L Street, NW
Washington, DC 20036-5687
(202) 429-1000
Fax: (202) 429-1293
webmaster@afscme.org
www.afscme.org

The activist newsletter of the American Federation of State, County and Municipal Employees.

AGAINST THE CURRENT

7012 Michigan Ave.
Detroit, MI 48210-2872
(313) 841-0160
Fax: (313) 841-8884
efc@igc.apc.org or solidarity@igc.org
www.igc.apc.org/solidarity

Published by Solidarity, this magazine promotes dialogue among activists, organizers and serious scholars of the left, from the general perspective of socialism from below.

AHORANOW

3780 Wilshire Blvd., Suite 1200
Los Angeles, CA 90010
(213) 387-2800 and (323) 387-3500
Fax: (213) 387-3500
laborctr@igc.org
www.thestrategycenter.org/AhoraNow/ahoranow.html

AhoraNow is a bilingual English/Spanish periodical of the Labor/Community Strategy Center, presenting left theory and practice. It documents corporate and government attacks against working people, giving primacy to voices from the front lines, and covers strategies and tactics in contemporary campaigns against racism and xenophobia.

AIM: ARMENIAN INTERNATIONAL MAGAZINE

207 S Brand Blvd., Suite 203
Glendale, CA 91204
(818) 246-7979
Fax: (818) 246-0088
www.armenianheritage.com/aimindex.htm

A monthly magazine of news and analysis about Armenia and the Armenian diaspora.

AKWESASNE NOTES
Mohawk Nation
P.O. Box 366
Roseveltown, NY 13683-0196
(518) 358-3326
Fax: (518) 358-3488
notes@glen-net.ca
www.ratical.org/AkwesasneNs.html

News of Mohawk and other indigenous peoples.

ALBION MONITOR
P.O. Box 1733
Sebastopol, CA 95473
(707) 823-0100
editor@monitor.net
www.monitor.net/monitor/0106a/default.html

AM is an online biweekly with a nationwide readership offering news and commentary from both alternative and mainstream sources, primarily covering environmental issues, human rights and politics. Its syndicated and other copyrighted material is available to subscribers only.

ALICE
1111 W El Camino Real #109 PMB 409
Sunnyvale, CA 94087
(650) 223-3335
Fax: (650) 745-8988
jsnnlsn@alicemagazine.com
www.alicemagazine.com

Alice: A magazine for women "on the other side of the looking glass."

ALLIANCE FOR COMMUNITY MEDIA
666 11th Street NW, Suite 740
Washington, DC 20001-45429
(202) 393-2650
Fax: (202) 393-2653
acm@alliancecm.org
www.alliancecm.org

This journal covers topics such as censorship, community and legal issues, and technical, professional and advocacy concerns for cable access, Internet and electronic media.

ALTERNATIVE PRESS REVIEW
P.O. BOX 4710
Arlington, VA 22204
(573) 442-4352
Fax: (703) 553-0565
editors@altpr.org
www.altpr.org

Published by A.A.L. Press, *APR* publishes a wide variety of the best essays from radical 'zines, tabloids, books and magazines and offers a selection of short and lively article excerpts along with reviews, commentary and columns on the alternative press scene and other alternative media.

ALTERNATIVE THERAPIES IN HEALTH AND MEDICINE

c/o InnoVision Communications, LLC
169 Saxony Rd., Suite 104
Encinitas, CA 92024
(866) 828-2962 or (760) 633-3910
Fax: (760) 633-3918
alttherapy@aol.com
www.alternative-therapies.com

Alternative Therapies in Health and Medicine shares information about the practical uses of alternative therapies in preventing and treating disease, healing illness and promoting health.

ALTERNATIVES JOURNAL

University of Waterloo, Faculty of Environmental Studies
Waterloo, ON N2L 3G1
Canada
(519) 888-4442 or (866) 437-2587
Fax: (519) 746-0292
info@alternativesjournal.ca
www.alternativesjournal.ca

As Canada's foremost environmental magazine, *Alternatives* offers engaging, thought-provoking articles on a wide range of environmental topics for activists, researchers and the casual reader alike.

AMERICAN EDITOR, THE

11690-B Sunrise Valley Dr.
Reston, VA 20191-1409
(703) 453-1122
Fax: (703) 453-1133
asne@asne.com
www.asne.org/kiosk/editor/tae.htm

Published by the American Society of Newspaper Editors, the *American Editor* discusses topics related to the current state and future of newspapers and journalism in this country.

AMERICAN HUMANIST ASSOCIATION, THE

1777 T Street NW
Washington, DC 20009-7125
(866) 486-2647
Fax: (202) 238-9003
AHA@erols.com
www.americanhumanist.org

The *AHA* represents both secular and religious naturalistic humanism, and cooperates with other national and international humanist organizations to advance the ideals of humanism.

AMERICAN JOURNALISM REVIEW

1117 Journalism Bldg.
College Park, MD 20742-7111
(301) 405-8323
Fax: (301) 405-8323
editor@ajr.umd.edu
www.ajr.org

American Journalism Review is a monthly, national magazine that covers trends in the industry: ethics and news in print, broadcast and online journalism.

AMERICAN LAWYER, THE

345 Park Ave.
New York, NY 10010
(800) 755-2773
Fax: (212) 481-8255
info@am/aw.com
www.americanlawyer.com

AL is the nation's leading legal monthly.

AMERICAN PROSPECT

5 Broad St.
Boston, MA 02109
(888) MUST-READ and (617) 547-2950
Fax: (617) 547-3896
letters@prospect.org
www.prospect.org

A bimonthly publication covering areas of concern such as political, social and cultural issues: "A journal for the liberal imagination."

AMERICAN WRITER

337 17th Street, #101
Oakland, CA 94612
(510) 839-0110
Fax: (510) 839-6097
nwu@nwu.org
www.nwu.org

Published by the National Writer's Union, *American Writer* reports on union activities and tracks developments in the media/information industry and the labor movement that concern working writers.

AMERICA'S FAMILY SUPPORT MAGAZINE

20 N. Wacker Dr., #1100
Chicago, IL 60606
(312) 338-0900
Fax: (312) 338-1522
info@familysupportamerica.org
www.familysupportamerica.org/content/afsm/afsmindex.htm

The journal of the nationally recognized movement to strengthen and support families and every setting in which children and families are present, *Family Support America* is part of the national strategy for ensuring the well-being of our children today and in years to come.

ANARCHO-SYNDICALIST REVIEW
P.O. BOX 2824
Champaign, IL 61825
jbekken@acad.suffolk.edu
flag.blackened.net/asr

ASR is the quarterly publication of revolutionary syndicalism.

ANARCHY: A JOURNAL OF DESIRE ARMED
P.O. Box 1446
Colombia, MO 65205-1446
(573) 442-4352
Fax: (573) 442-4352
jmcquinn@coin.org
www.anarchymag.org

An international magazine for anarchist resistance by C.A.L. Press, *Anarchy* is neither left nor right, just uncompromisingly anti-authoritarian, radically co-operative and communitarian, ecological and feminist.

ANIMAL PEOPLE
P.O. Box 960
Clinton, WA 98236-0960
(360) 579-2505
anmlpepl@whidbey.com
www.animalpeoplenews.org

Animal People is the leading independent newspaper and electronic information service providing original investigation of animal protection worldwide.

ANIMALS' AGENDA, THE
P.O. Box 25881
Baltimore, MD 21224
(410) 675-4566
Fax: (410) 675-0066
office@animalsagenda.org
www.animalsagenda.org

The Animals' Agenda is a quarterly news magazine dedicated to informing people about animal rights and cruelty-free living for the purpose of inspiring action for animals. *The Animals' Agenda* is committed to serving—and fostering co-operation among—a combined audience of animal advocates, interested individuals and the entire animal rights movement.

ANNALS OF IMPROBABLE RESEARCH
P.O. Box 380853
Cambridge, MA 02238
(617) 491-4437
Fax: (617) 661-0927
marca@chem2.harvard.edu
www.improb.com

AIR is a humor magazine about science, technology and medicine. AIR also produces the annual IG Nobel Prize Ceremony, honoring people whose achievements cannot or should not be reproduced.

ANTIPODE
350 Main St.
Malden, MA 02148
(781) 388-8200
Fax: (781) 388-8210
newmedia@blackwellpublishers.co.uk
www.blackwellpublishers.co.uk/asp/
journal.asp?ref=0066-4812&src=aim

For thirty years *Antipode* has been
the place to publish radical scholarship in geography. This radical journal of geography, published by
Blackwell, attracts the best and
most provocative of radical geographical theory and research, particularly that which contributes to
politics and practice.

APPALACHIAN READER
1129 Burton Rd.
Knoxville, TN 37919
(865) 212-3509
jamiedsign@aol.com
www.appalachianreader.org/About.html

The *Appalachian Reader* covers the
work of citizens' organizations and
others working for justice in the
region. It also provides information
about job openings; publicizes
resources and foundations that support organizations in the region; and
covers the activities of locals.

ARAB AMERICAN NEWS
5706 Chase Rd.
Dearborn, MI 48126
(313) 582-4888
Fax: (313) 582-7870
osibilani@aol.com
www.arabamericannews.com

The *Arab American News* is a
nationally circulated, bilingual
weekly newspaper serving the
nation's three million Arab
Americans.

ARK, THE
715 G Street SE
Washington, DC 20003
(202) 543-6603
Fax: (202) 543-2462
info@noacentral.org
www.noacentral.org

ARMS SALES MONITOR
1717 K Street NW, Suite 209
Washington, DC 20036
(202) 546-3300 ext. 193
Fax: (202)675-1010
tamarg@fas.org
www.fas.org/asmp

Published by the Federation of
American Scientists, *Arms Sales
Monitor* highlights U.S. government
policies on arms exports and conventional weapons proliferation.

ARSENAL

1573 N Milwaukee Ave, #420
Chicago, IL 60622
arsenal@wwa.com
www.azone.org/arsenalmag/index.html

Arsenal: "A Magazine of Anarchist
Strategy and Culture."

ASHEVILLE GLOBAL REPORT

P.O. Box 1504
Asheville, NC 28802
(828) 236-3103
editors@agrnews.org
www.agrnews.org/issues/130/index.
html

Asheville Global Report covers
news underreported by mainstream
media so as to provide the free
exchange of information vital for
social change.

ASIAN REPORTER, THE

922 N Killingsworth St., Suite 1-A
Portland, OR 97217-2220
(503) 283-4440
Fax: (503) 283-4445
asianreporter@juno.com
www.asianreporter.com

This Pacific Northwest–based weekly features national, international
and local news and events with an
Asian focus.

ASIANWEEK

809 Sacramento St.
San Francisco, CA 94108
(415) 397-0220
Fax: (415) 397-7258
asianweek@asianweek.com
www.asianweek.com

AsianWeek is a nationally circulated publication with a community
focus, covering news of Asian-
Americans.

BAFFLER, THE

P.O. Box 378293
Chicago, IL 60637
(888) 387-8947
Fax: (773) 493-0515
info@thebaffler.org
www.thebaffler.org

The *Baffler* is an independent journal of cultural criticism and literature. Great writing, often humorous.

BAMBOO GIRL

P.O. Box 507
New York, NY 10159-0507
(212) 894-3748 x3387
bamboogirl@aol.com
www.bamboogirl.com/index.html

Bamboo Girl challenges the issues
of racism/sexism/homophobia from
the point of view of smart, loud,
nontraditional girls of color, especially from that of the pro-female,
Filipina/Asian.

BEAT WITHIN, THE
660 Market St.
San Francisco, CA 94104
(415) 438-4755
pacificnews@pacificnews.org
www.pacificnews.org/yo/beat

The Beat Within is a weekly newsletter of writing and art by incarcerated youth published by Pacific News Service.

BIG WORLD MAGAZINE
P.O. Box 7656-H
Lancaster, PA 17604-8743
(888) 550-7264
Fax: (810) 277-8376 and (717) 569-0217
bigworld@bigworld.com
www.bigworld.com/

A fresh, unpretentious quarterly magazine that celebrates the simple joy of independent travel—and steers clear of corporate, sterile luxury.

BITCH:FEMINIST RESPONSE TO POP CULTURE
2765 16th Street
San Francisco, CA 94103
(415) 864-6671
Fax: (415) 503-0142
bitch@bitchmagazine.com
www.bitchmagazine.com

Devoted to feminist analysis of movies, television, advertising and sociocultural trends, *Bitch* also spotlights women making alternative, progressive media.

BLACK ENTERPRISE
130 5th Avenue
New York, NY 10011
(212) 242-8000
Fax: (212) 886-9610
interactive@blackenterprise.com
www.blackenterprise.com

The authority on business news, strategies, information and resources for African-American entrepreneurs, corporate executives, managers and professionals, this monthly magazine provides essential business and financial information.

BLACK ISSUES IN HIGHER EDUCATION
10520 Warwick Ave., Suite B-8
Fairfax, VA 22030-3136
(703) 385-2981 and (800) 783-3199
Fax: (703) 385-1839
www.blackissues.com

Published biweekly, *Black Issues in Higher Education* is the nation's only news magazine dedicated exclusively to minority issues in higher education.

BLACK MASKS
P.O. Box 2, Riverdale Station
Bronx, NY 10471
(212) 304-8900

met1@is.nyu.edu
www.blackmasks.com

One of the most extensive bimonthly publications devoted to black performing and visual arts in the United States.

BLACK PARENTING TODAY

P.O. Box 28663
Philadelphia, PA 19151
bptmag@earthlink.net
www.blackparentingtoday.org/editors.html

Geared toward those who are actively involved in raising African-American children, *Black Parenting Today* is working with other parents, making the neighborhoods safer, and strengthening and educating the community—and the next generation of black leaders—across the board.

BLACK RENAISSANCE/ RENAISSANCE NOIRE

601 N Morton St.
Bloomington, IN 47404
(800) 842-6796
Fax: (812) 855-8507
black.renaissance@nyu.edu.
iupjournals.org/blackren

Published three times a year, *Black Renaissance/Renaissance Noire* publishes essays, fiction, reviews and art work that address the full range of contemporary black concerns

BLACK SCHOLAR

P.O. Box 2869
Oakland, CA 94618-0069
(510) 547-6633
Fax: (510) 547-6679
blkschlr@aol.com
www.theblackscholar.org
An independent intellectual journal of the African-American experience.

BLACK WORLD TODAY, THE

P.O. Box 328
Randallstown, MD 21133
(410) 521-4678 or (410) 539-TBWT
Fax: (410) 521-9993
editors@tbwt.net
www.tbwt.com

"We are a collective of journalists, writers, artists, communicators and entrepreneurs who have banded together to use the information revolution as one means towards the overall empowerment of black people in the United States and around the world."

BLACKWELL PUBLISHERS
350 Main St.
Malden, MA 02148
(781) 388-8200
Fax: (781) 388-8210
imcla@blackwellpub.com
www.blackwellpub.com

Blackwell publishes Marxist, socialist, anarchist, anti-racist and feminist analyses of environmental and geographical issues.

BLK
P.O. Box 83912
Los Angeles, CA 90083-0912
(310) 410-0808
Fax: (310) 410-9250
newsroom@blk.com
www.blk.com

BLK is a news magazine for the black lesbian and gay community.

BOCA MAGAZINE
P.O. Box 862246
Los Angeles, CA 90210
(323) 225-6000
Fax: (323) 225-6566
boca@bocamagazine.com
www.bocamagazine.com

The true alternative voice of Latinos in the L.A., *BOCA* is read predominantly by college-educated Raza because it speaks to their experiences of growing up and living in Southern California.

BOSTON REVIEW
E53-407, MIT
Cambridge, MA 02139
(617) 253-3642
Fax: (617) 252-1549
bostonreview@mit.edu
www.bostonreview.org

Boston Review combines commitments to public reason with literary imagination.

BRAIN CHILD: THE MAGAZINE FOR THINKING MOTHERS
P.O. Box 714
Lexington, VA 24450
(540) 463-4817
publisher@brainchildmag.com
www.brainchildmag.com

Brain Child is a quarterly print publication that reflects modern motherhood.

BRAZZIL
2039 North Ave.
Los Angeles, CA 90042-1024
(213) 255-8062
Fax: (213) 257-3487
brazzil@brazzil.com
www.brazzil.com

This monthly features in-depth articles dealing with politics, economy, behavior, ecology, tourism, literature, arts and culture in general. The magazine has a national calendar of events and features "That's

Brazilian," a list of Brazilian businesses in all major cities throughout the United States.

BRIARPATCH
2138 McIntyre St.
Regina, SK S4P 2R7
Canada
(306) 525-2949
Fax: (306) 565-3430
briarpatch.mag@sasktel.net
www.briarpatchmagazine.com

Briarpatch, "Saskatchewan's Independent News Magazine," reports alternative views on politics, labor and international events.

BROADCASTING AND CABLE MAGAZINE
P.O. Box 15157
North Hollywood, CA 91615-5157
(800) 554-5729
smcclellan@cahners.com
www.broadcastingcable.com

A newsweekly on broadcasting and cable issues.

BROKEN PENCIL
P.O. Box 203, Station P
Toronto, ON M5S 2S7
Canada
(416) 538-2813
editor@brokenpencil.com
www.brokenpencil.com

This "guide to alternative culture in Canada" reviews the best 'zines, books, Web sites, videos, and artworks from the underground and reprints the best articles from the alternative press. *Broken Pencil* also publishes ground breaking interviews, original fiction and commentary on all aspects of the independent arts.

BULLETIN OF THE ATOMIC SCIENTISTS
6042 S Kimbark Ave.
Chicago, IL 60637
(773) 702-2555
Fax: (773) 702-0725
bulletin@thebulletin.org
www.bullatomsci.org

Published by the Education Foundation for Nuclear Science since 1947, this bimonthly "Magazine of Global Security News And Analysis" covers international security, military affairs and nuclear issues.

BUSINESS ETHICS
Insider's Report on Responsible Business
P.O. Box 8439
Minneapolis, MN 55408
(612) 879-0695
Fax: (612) 879-0699
BizEthics@aol.com
www.business-ethics.com

Aiming to promote ethical business practices, *BE* includes socially responsible business and investment news, information and management ideas; insightful editorials; book reviews; and progressive economics.

BY WHAT AUTHORITY
P.O. Box 246
South Yarmouth, MA 02664-0246
(508) 398-1145
Fax: (508) 398-1552
people@poclad.org
www.poclad.org

A publication of the Program on Corporations, Law & Democracy (POCLAD).

CABINET MAGAZINE
181 Wyckoff St.
Brooklyn, NY 11217
(718) 222-8434
Fax: (718) 222-3700
info@immaterial.net
www.cabinetmagazine.org

Cabinet is a quarterly magazine of international art and culture. The magazine contains articles, interviews, specially commissioned artist projects, a free CD or CD-ROM every second issue, and a special 16-page section around a particular theme.

CALIFORNIA PRISON FOCUS
2940 16th Street, #307
San Francisco, CA 94103
(415) 252-9211
Fax: (415) 252-9311
info@prisons.org
www.prisons.org

California Prison Focus is a newsletter that reports on control unit prisons, conditions in California and provides a voice for prisoners.

CALIFORNIA WILD
California Academy of Sciences
Golden Gate Park
San Francisco, CA 94118
(415) 750-7117
Fax: (415) 221-4853
calwild@calacademy.org
www.calacademy.org/calwild

A project of the California Academy of Sciences, the magazine has adjusted its focus to encompass discussion of the causes and ramifications of environmental degradation and the rapid decline in biodiversity.

CALYPSO LOG
870 Greenbrier Circle, Suite 402
Chesapeake, VA 23320
(800) 441-4395
Fax: (757) 523-2747
cousteau@cousteausociety.org
www.cousteau.org

This journal of the Cousteau Society focuses on protection and improvement of the quality of life for future generations.

CANADIAN DIMENSION
2B-91 Albert St.
Winnipeg, MB R3B 1G5
Canada
(800) 737-7051
Fax: (204) 943-4617
info@canadiandimension.mb.ca
www.canadiandimension.mb.ca

For thirty-five years *CD* has been a source of information and inspiration for activists and intellectuals on the left, offering principled and independent hard news and analysis from a left-wing perspective. A magazine "For People Who Want to Change the World," it is the recipient of multiple Project Censored Canada awards.

CAPITAL EYE
1101 14th Street NW, Suite 1030
Washington, DC 20005-5635
(202) 857-0044
Fax: (202) 857-7809
info@crp.org
www.crp.org

This quarterly of the Center for Responsive Politics aims to educate its readers and to encourage them to examine the role of money in the U.S. political system. It includes substantive, topical articles on issues related to money and politics.

CAREER COMMUNICATIONS GROUP INC.
Black Family Network
729 E Pratt St., 5th Floor
Baltimore, MD 21202
(410) 244-7101
Fax: (410) 752-1837
www.ccgmag.com
www.blackfamilynet.net

This quarterly dedicated to promoting opportunities for black Americans in business provides interviews with successful minorities in business and education, offering a balanced and realistic portrayal of minority Americans' growing role in business.

CENSORSHIP NEWS
275 7th Avenue, 20th Floor
New York, NY 10001
(212) 807-6222
Fax: (212) 807-6245
ncac@ncac.org
www.ncac.org

Published quarterly, this journal of the National Coalition Against Censorship contains information and discussion about freedom of expression issues, including current school censorship controversies and threats to the free flow of information.

CHALLENGE
P.O. Box 41199
Jaffa 61411
Israel
972-3-6839145
Fax: 972-3-6839148
oda@netvision.net.il
www.odaction.org/challenge

This publication is directed to those members of the international community seeking a critical and accurate presentation of the dramatic events in the region.

CHANGE LINKS
P.O. Box 9682
North Hollywood, CA 91609-1682
(818) 982-1422
change@pacbell.net
www.change-links.org

This progressive newspaper and calendar is distributed nationally and locally in the L.A. area.

CHICAGO REPORTER
332 S. Michigan Ave., Suite 500
Chicago, IL 60604
(312) 427-4830 x221
Fax: (312) 427-6130
editor@chicagoreporter.com
www.chicagoreporter.com

Chicago Reporter focuses on issues of race and poverty.

CHRISTIAN SCIENCE MONITOR
Journal of The First Church of Christ, Scientist
1 Norway St.
Boston, MA 02115-3195
(617) 450-2000
orders@csmonitor.com
www.csmonitor.com

This 87-year-old daily newspaper covers national and international news.

CHRONICLE OF HIGHER EDUCATION, THE
1255 23rd Street NW, Suite 700
Washington, DC 20037
(202) 466-1000
Fax: (202) 296-2691
help@chronicle.com
www.chronicle.com

The number one news source for college and university faculty about issues in higher education.

CHRONICLE OF PHILANTHROPY, THE
1255 23rd Street NW, 7th Floor
Washington, DC 20037
(202) 466-1200
Fax: (202) 466-2078
editor@philanthropy.com
www.philanthropy.com

The *Chronicle of Philanthropy* is the newspaper of the nonprofit world. Published bimonthly, it is the number one news source for charity leaders, fund raisers, grant makers, and other people involved in the philanthropic enterprise.

CINEASTE

P.O. Box 2242
New York, NY 10009-8917
(212) 366-5720
Fax: (212) 366-5724
cineaste@cineaste.com
www.cineaste.com

A quarterly of the art and politics of the cinema.

CINEMAN SYNDICATE

P.O. Box 4433
Middletown, NY 10940-8301
(845) 692-4572
Fax: (845) 692-8311
cineman@frontiernet.net
www.frontiernet.net/~cineman

Established in 1975 to provide capsule movie reviews to newspapers, this multi-ethnic weekly has now expanded to feature book reviews, music reviews, box office reports and star interviews.

CIVIL LIBERTIES

125 Broad St., 18th Floor
New York, NY 10004-2400
(212) 549-2500
Fax: (212) 549-2646
nauer@citylimits.org
www.aclu.org

Published by the American Civil Liberties Union, it covers issues of civil liberties and includes online information on Internet free speech issues.

CLAMOR

P.O. Box 1225
Bowling Green, OH 43402
(419) 353-8266
info@clamormagazine.org
www.clamormagazine.org

This new bimonthly magazine published by Become The Media brings you the depth of the human experience without the corporate filters, providing new perspectives on politics, culture, media and life.

CMYK MAGAZINE

5B Isadora Duncan Lane
San Francisco, CA 94102
info@cmykmag.com
www.cmykmag.com

CMYK:The Future of Creative was launched in May of 1996 as a much-needed showcase of outstanding student work in advertising, design, illustration and photography.

COLORLINES MAGAZINE
formerly Third Force
PMB 319, 4096 Piedmont Ave.
Oakland, CA 94611
(510) 653-3415
Fax: (510) 653-3427
colorlines@arc.org
www.arc.org

This the quarterly journal of the Applied Research Center and Center for Third World Organizing focuses on race, culture and organizing within communities of color.

COLUMBIA JOURNALISM REVIEW
Columbia University
Journalism Building
2950 Broadway
New York, NY 10027
(212) 854-1881
Fax: (212) 854-8580
info@cjr.org
www.cjr.org

This review assesses the performance of journalists and stimulates continuing improvements in the profession.

COMET MAGAZINE
3388 22nd Street
San Francisco, CA 94110
(510) 526-5922
cometmagazine@hotmail.com
www.cometmagazine.net

Comet Magazine supports independent art and literature and features interviews and articles about people with new ideas and solutions to artistic and cultural dilemmas.

COMMUNITIES MAGAZINE
138-W Twin Oaks Rd.
P.O. Box 169
Louisa, VA 23093
(800) 462-8240
Fax: (970) 593-5615
communities@igc.org
fic.ic.org/cmag

Communities Magazine focuses on intentional communities, including ecovillages, co-housing, urban housing co-operatives, shared living and other projects.

COMMUNITY MEDIA REVIEW
Alliance for Community Media
666 11th Street NW, Suite 740
Washington, DC 20001-4542
(202) 393-2650
Fax: (202) 393-2653
acm@alliancecm.org
http://world.std.com/~MaldenTV/cmr/index.html

This journal of the Alliance for Community Media reports on political and regulatory issues in the media and emerging information systems.

COMPARATIVE STUDIES OF SOUTH AFRICA, ASIA, & THE MIDDLE EAST
Duke University Press, Journal Division
P.O. Box 90660
Durham, NC 90660
(888) 387-5765
Fax: (888) 651-0124
subscriptions@dukeupress.edu
dukeupress.edu/journals/index.shtml

This semiannual journal explores the shared concerns and histories of the said regions, offers stimulating perspectives on interdisciplinary debates, and challenges established analytic models.

CONGRESSIONAL QUARTERLY WEEKLY REPORT
1414 22nd Street NW
Washington, DC 20036
(202) 887-8500
Fax: (202)728-1863
customer service@cq.com
www.cq.com

This publication provides world-class reportage on issues of government, politics and public policy.

CONSCIOUS CHOICE
Journal of Ecology and Natural Living
920 North Franklin St. Suite 202
Chicago, IL 60610-3119
(312) 440-4373

Fax: (312) 751-3973
cc@consciouschoice.com or
aliess@consciouschoice.com
www.consciouschoice.com

Conscious Choice promotes sustainable patterns of living; environmental issues; vegetarian nutrition; and natural alternatives, health and lifestyles.

CONSUMER REPORTS
101 Truman Ave.
Yonkers, NY 10703-1057
(914) 378-2000
Fax: (914) 378-2992
www.consumerreports.org

The oldest, most reliable and complete source for independent reviews of products and services, this report is produced by Consumer's Union, a nonprofit organization that has been testing products on behalf of consumers for more than sixty years.

CO-OP AMERICA QUARTERLY
1612 K Street NW, Suite 600
Washington, DC 20006
(800) 58-GREEN and (202) 872-5307
Fax: (202) 331-8166
info@coopamerica.org
www.coopamerica.org

Published by Co-op America, this quarterly teaches consumers how to use their spending power to support socially and environmentally responsible businesses and promote social and economic justice.

CORPORATE CRIME REPORTER
1209 National Press Building
Washington, DC 20045
(202) 737-1680
russell@essential.org.

This legal weekly covers issues of corporate and white-collar crime.

COUNTER MEDIA
1573 N Milwaukee Ave., #517
Chicago, IL 60622
(312) 243-8342
lquilter@igc.apa.org

Counter Media covers protests, actions and issues ignored by conventional media sources.

COUNTERPOISE
1716 SW Williston Rd.
Gainesville, FL 32608-4049
(352) 335-2200
Fax: call first
willet@liblib.com
www.civicmediacenter.org/counterpoise

Counterpoise: Quarterly Journal of the American Library Association's Social Responsibilities Round Table is the only review journal that makes alternative points of view widely accessible to librarians, scholars and activists.

COUNTERPUNCH
3220 N Street NW, Suite 346
Washington, DC 20007
(800) 840-3683
counterpunch@counterpunch.org
www.counterpunch.org

Twice a month *Counterpunch* brings its readers the stories that the corporate press never prints. Theirs is muckraking with a radical attitude.

COVERTACTION QUARTERLY
c/o Institute for Media Analysis, Inc.
143 West 4th Street
New York, NY 10012
(212) 477-2977
Fax: (212) 477-2977
Info@covertaction.org
www.covertaction.org

CAQ offers investigative journalism exposing malfeasance and covert activities in government, corporations and other areas affecting the public.

CRITICAL ASIAN STUDIES
(Formerly the Bulletin of Concerned Asian Scholars)
3693 South Bay Bluffs Dr.
Cedar, MI 49621
(231) 228-7116
Fax: (253) 540-2583
tfenton@igc.org
csf.Colorado.edu/bcas

A major U.S. journal on sociopolitical concerns in modern Asia.

CUBA UPDATE
124 West 23rd Street
New York, NY 10011
(212) 242-0559
Fax: (212) 242-1937
cubanctr@igc.org
www.cubaupdate.org

Cuba Update, published by the
Center for Cuban Studies, provides
accurate, accessible news coverage
and discussion of important issues
almost impossible to find elsewhere.

CULTURAL SURVIVAL
QUARTERLY (CSQ)
215 Prospect St.
Cambridge, MA 02139
(617) 441-5400
Fax: (617) 441-5417
csinc@cs.org
www.cs.org

This quarterly magazine is based on
the belief that the survival of indigenous people and ethnic minorities
depends on their rights to decide
how to adapt traditional ways to a
changing world.

CURVE MAGAZINE
1 Haight St., Suite B
San Francisco, CA 94102
(415) 863-6538
Fax: (415) 863-1609
shop@curvemag.com
www.curvemag.com

Curve, the nations best selling lesbian magazine, spotlights all that is
fresh, funny, or controversial in the
lesbian community alongside entertainment profiles and investigative
pieces.

DARK NIGHT FIELD NOTES
P.O. Box 3629
Chicago, IL 60690-3629
(207) 839-5794
Fax: (773) 373-7188
darknight@igc.org
www.darknightpress.org

Published quarterly by Dark Night
Press, this magazine covers issues
related to the recognition and liberation of indigenous peoples

DEAL WITH IT
P.O. Box 5841
Eugene, OR 97405
dealewithit@fruitiondesign.com
www.fruitiondesign.com/dealwithit

This bimonthly journal is put out
by anti-sexist anarchist men in support of the struggle to end sexist
oppression, deconstruct gender,
overthrow patriarchy and acheive
total liberation.

DEFENSE MONITOR
1779 Massachusetts Ave. NW, 6th
Floor
Washington, DC 20036
(202) 332-0600
Fax: (202) 462-4559
info@cdi.org
www.cdi.org

Defense Monitor provides independent research on the social, economic, environmental, political and military components of global security.

DEMOCRATIC LEFT
180 Varick St., 12th Floor
New York, NY 10014
(212) 727-8610
Fax: (212)727-8616
dsa@dsausa.org
www.dsausa.org/dl/index.html

Published by the Democratic Socialists of America, this quarterly review examines socialist issues and activities.

DESIGNER/BUILDER
2405 Maclovia Lane
Santa Fe, NM 87505
(505) 471-4549
Fax: Same
www.designerbuildermagazine.com

Published twelve times a year by Fine Additions Inc., *Designer/Builder* is a journal of the human environment.

DISSENT MAGAZINE
310 Riverside Dr., Suite 1201
New York, NY 10025
(212) 316-3120
Fax: (212) 316-3145
editors@dissentmagazine.org
www.dissentmagazine.org

A quarterly magazine of politics, culture and ideas, *Dissent* covers national and international politics from a progressive perspective with a focus on providing forums for debate, disagreement and discussion on the left.

DIVERSECITY: A QUEENS MULTICULTURAL NEWSPAPER
43-13 47th St., Suite E36
Sunnyside, NY 11104
(718) 937-8185
dennis@newhumanist.net
www.centerofcultures.org/newspaper

This publication serves as a platform for a dynamic mosaic of cultures.

DIVERSITY: CAREER OPPORTUNITIES AND INSIGHT
1800 Sherman Ave., Suite 404
Evanston, IL 60201-3769
(847) 448-1019
Fax: (847) 475-8807
vicki.chong@careermedia.com

This national equal-opportunity journal addresses the career development needs of today's diverse, professional multi-ethnic workforce.

DIVERSITY SUPPLIERS & BUSINESS MAGAZINE
P.O. Box 579
Winchester, CA 92596
(909) 926-2119

This trade magazine addresses the varied and complex issues vital to the suppliers and purchasers of diverse businesses.

DOLLARS AND SENSE: WHAT'S LEFT IN ECONOMICS
740 Cambridge St.
Cambridge, MA 02141-1401
(617) 876-2434
Fax: (617) 876-0008
dollars@dollarsandsense.org
www.dollarsandsense.org

Published by the Economic Affairs Bureau, *Dollars and Sense* reports on issues of social justice and economic policy and presents articles by journalists, activists and scholars on a broad range of economic topics.

DOMES
P.O. Box 413
Milwaukee, WI 53211
(414) 229-4709
Fax: (414) 229-4848
info@sois.uwm.edu
www.sois.uwm.edu

This biannual provides for a balance of views on the Middle East.

DOUBLE TAKE
55 Davis Square
Somerville, MA 02144
(617) 591-9389
dtmag@doubletakemagazine.org
www.doubletakemagazine.org

Quarterly magazine of fiction, poetry and the documentary arts.

E: THE ENVIRONMENTAL MAGAZINE
P.O. Box 5098
Westport, CT 06881
(203) 854-5559
Fax: (203) 866-0602
info@emagazine.com
emagazine.com

E is an independent newsstand-quality publication that focuses on environmental issues. E strives to educate, inspire and empower Americans to make a difference for the environment.

EARTH FIRST! JOURNAL
P.O. Box 3023
Tucson, AZ 85702-6900
(520) 620-6900
Fax: (413) 254-0057
collective@earthfirstjournal.org
www.earthfirstjournal.org

Earth First! Journal reports on the radical environmental movement. The journal publishes hard-to-find information about strategies to stop the destruction of the planet.

EARTH ISLAND JOURNAL
300 Broadway St., Suite 28
San Francisco, CA 94133-3312
(415) 788-3666
Fax: (415) 788-7324
journal@earthisland.org
earthisland.org/

Earth Island is an international environmental news magazine focusing on socio-economic and political issues affecting ecosystems and on the work being done to conserve, preserve and restore the Earth.

EARTHLIGHT MAGAZINE
111 Fairmount Ave.
Oakland, CA 94611
(510) 451-4926
klauren@earthlight.org
www.earthlight.org

Earthlight is the magazine to read if you are concerned about the fate of the planet and have a sense that, at its root, this issue is a profoundly spiritual. Published quarterly, *Earthlight:The Magazine of Spiritual Ecology* presents lively articles from a wide spectrum of thinkers in touch with the cutting edge of ecological consciousness.

ECOLOGIST, THE
c/o MIT Press Journals
1920 Martin Luther King, Jr. Blvd.
Berkeley, CA 94704
(510) 548-2032
Fax: (510) 548-4916
theecologist@earthlink.net
www.theecologist.org

Produced monthly, the *Ecologist*, now in its 33rd year, is the world's longest running environmental magazine. It highlights campaigns on the environment and social issues facing this planet.

ECONOMIC JUSTICE NEWS
3628 12th Street NE
Washington, DC 20017
(202) 463-2265
Fax: (202) 879-3186
50years@50years.org
www.50years.org

Economic Justice News is the quarterly newsletter produced by the 50 Years Is Enough Network, a network of 200 social and economic justice organizations working to bring about radical reform of the World Bank and the International Monetary Fund.

EIDOS MAGAZINE

P.O. Box 990095 Prudentia Center
Station
Boston, MA 02199-0095
(617) 262-0096
Fax: (617) 364-0096
eidos@eidos.org
www.eidos.org

Eidos advocates and defends sexual
freedom as a human, constitutional
and civil right.

EL ANDAR

P.O. Box 7745
Santa Cruz, CA 95061
(831) 457-8353 or 831-460-9910
Fax: (831) 457-8354
info@elandar.com
www.elandar.com

*El Andar: A Latino Magazine for the
New Millenium* is an award-winning publication focusing on Latino
issues.

EL INFORMADOR HISPANO

3722 Decatur Ave.
Fort Worth, TX 76106
(817) 626-8624
Fax: (817) 626-8635
elinfohispan@aol

This publication promotes professional development of the Latino
media in the United States.

EL MUNDO

630 20th Street
Oakland, CA 94612
(510) 287-8223
Fax: (510) 763-9670
malpave@aol.com or
vsw@citycom.com

A national Spanish-language publication.

EL SALVADOR WATCH

19 West 21st Street, Room 502
New York, NY 10010
(212) 465-8115
Fax: (212) 465-8998
cispesnatl@people-link.com
www.cispes.org

Published by Committee in Solidarity
with the People of El Salvador, *El
Salvador Watch* is the newsletter of
this grassroots organization dedicated
to supporting the Salvadoran people's
struggle for self-determination and
social and economic justice.

EL VISTAZO

1376 North 4th Street
San Jose, CA 95112
(408) 436-7850
Fax: (408) 436-7861
laoferta@bayarea.net
www.laoferta.com

El Vistazo is the most awarded
bilingual newspaper in the United
States.

ELECTRONIC JOURNALIST, THE
3909 N Meridian St.
Indianapolis, IN 46208
(317) 927-8000
Fax: (317) 920-4789
spj@spj.org
www.spj.org

TEC, published by the Society of Professional Journalists, is a national magazine dedicated to improving and protecting journalism.

ENVIRONMENTAL HEALTH MONTHLY
P.O. Box 6806
Falls Church, VA 22040
(703) 237-2249
Fax: (703) 237-8389
info@chej.org
www.chej.org

This monthly digest of reprinted environmental, medical and scientific articles is published by the Center for Health, Environment and Justice.

ESSENCE MAGAZINE
1500 Broadway
New York, NY 10036
(212) 642-0600
Fax: (212) 921-5173
www.essence.com

News and commentary for African-American women.

EVERYBODY'S: THE CARIBBEAN-AMERICAN MAGAZINE
1630 Nostrand Ave.
Brooklyn, NY 11226
(718) 941-1879
Fax: (718) 941-1886
everybodys@msn.com
www.caribbeansports.com/ebm/
    ebm.html

This general interest Caribbean-American monthly magazine focuses on issues affecting the diverse ethnicities and nationalities in the Caribbean-American community.

EVERYONE'S BACKYARD
P.O. Box 6806
Falls Church, VA 22040-6806
(703) 237-2249
Fax: (703) 237-8389
info@chej.org
www.chej.org

Published by the Center for Health, Environment and Justice, Everyone's Backyard is the journal of the Grassroots Movement for Environmental Justice.

EXTRA!
112 West 27th Street
New York, NY 10001
(212) 633-6700
Fax: (212) 727-7668
info@fair.org
www.fair.org

Published by Fairness and Accuracy in Reporting, EXTRA! provides media criticism and features articles on biased reporting, censored news, media mergers and more.

F.A.C.T.NET NEWSLETTER
P.O. Box 3135
Boulder, CO 80307-3135
factnet@factnet.org
www.factnet.org

The newsletter of F.A.C.T.Net (Fight Against Coercive Tactics Network) is a nonprofit news source, referral service and archive. It is the oldest and largest cult and mind control resource on the Internet, dedicated to protecting freedom of mind from harms caused by psychological coercion.

FACTSHEET 5
P.O. Box 170099
San Francisco, CA 94117-0099
(415) 668-1781
seth@factsheet5.com
www.factsheet5.com

This guide to the 'zine revolution offers resources and reviews of thousands of underground publications.

FAT!SO?
P.O. Box 423464
San Francisco, CA 94142-3464
(800) OHFATSO
marilyn@fatso.com
www.fatso.com

The magazine for people who don't apologize for their size.

FELLOWSHIP MAGAZINE
P.O. Box 271
Nyack, NY 10960
(845) 358-4601
Fax: (845) 358-4924
for@forusa.org
www.forusa.org

Published by the Fellowship of Reconciliation, *Fellowship Magazine* seeks to replace violence, war, racism and economic injustice with nonviolence, peace and justice.

FEMINIST MAJORITY REPORT
1600 Wilson Blvd. #801
Arlington, VA 22209
(703) 522-2214
Fax: (703) 522-2219
www.feminist.org

News and reports on politics, culture, women's health, reproductive rights, events, career opportunities and the multidimensional nature of feminism.

FILIPINAS MAGAZINE
1486 Huntington Ave., Suite 300
South San Francisco, CA 94080
(800) 654-777
Fax: (650) 872-8651
mail@filipinasmag.com
www.filipinasmag,com

This monthly covers Filipino-American interests and affairs, with both the immigrant and U.S.-born sectors of the more than two million Filipinos in this country as its audience. The magazine focuses on achievers, role models, politics and issues both in the United States and the Philippines.

FILIPINO EXPRESS, THE
2711 Kennedy Blvd.
Jersey City, NJ 07306
(201) 434-1114
Fax: (201) 434-0880
filexpress@aol.com
www.filipinoexpress.com

A nationally distributed weekly with news of the Asia-Pacific Islands.

FILIPINO REPORTER
350 5th Avenue, Suite 601 Empire State Bldg.
New York, NY 10018-0110
(212) 967-5784
Fax: (212) 967-5848
FilipinoReporter@worldnet.att.net
BPelayo@aol.com
www.filipinoreporter.com

A national English-language weekly of particular interest to Asians and Pacific Islanders.

FIRE INSIDE, THE
100 McAllister St.
San Francisco, CA 94102
(415) 255-7036 x4
Fax: (415) 552-3150
ccwp@igc.org
www.prisonactivist.org/ccwp

Published by California Coalition for Women Prisoners, this quarterly newsletter covers issues related to incarcerated women.

FOOD FIRST NEWS
Institute for Food and Development Policy
398 60th Street.
Oakland, CA 94618
(510) 654-4400
Fax: (510) 654-4400
foodfirst@igc.apc.org
www.foodfirst.org

Food First News offers information and and a reader action-guide for ending world hunger and poverty.

FOOD NOT BOMBS MENU
P.O. Box 744
Tucson, AZ 85702
(800) 884-1136
foodnotbombs@earthlink.net

The menu reprints flyers, letters
and news reports about Food
Not Bombs, Homes Not Jails,
the free radio movement and
other elements of the direct
action community.

FOREIGN AFFAIRS
P.O. Box 420235
Palm Coast, FL 32142-0235
(800) 829.5539
foraff@palmcoastd.com
www.foreignaffairs.org

Approaching its 75th year, *Foreign
Affairs*, published by the Council on
Foreign Relations, is still at the fore-
front of serious discussion of the
world and of the role of the United
States in it; publishing authors of
widely divergent views it searches
for unifying themes and principles
in an era where these are especially
hard to find.

FOREST MAGAZINE
P.O. Box 11646
Eugene, OR 97440
(541) 484-2692
info@forestmag.org
www.forestmag.org

Conserving our national heritage,
Forest Magazine is for people who
care about forests.

FORWARD NEWSPAPER
45 East 33rd Street
New York, NY 10016
(212) 889-8200
Fax: 447-6406
acaroll@forward.com
www.forward.com

The weekly national *Forward* fought
for social justice and helped generations of immigrant Jews enter
American life—and it still does.

FREE INQUIRY: THE INTERNATIONAL SECULAR HUMANIST MAGAZINE
P.O. Box 664
Amherst, NY 14226
(716) 636-7571
Fax: (716) 636-1733
www.secularhumanism.org

Published by the Council for Secular
Humanism, FI is a quarterly magazine that celebrates reason and
humanity.

FREEDOM SOCIALIST NEWSPAPER

4710 University Way NE #100
Seattle, WA 981045
(206) 985-4621
Fax: (206) 985-8965
fspnatl@igc.apc.org
www.socialism.com

Published by Revolutionary Feminist
Internationalists, this international
socialist feminist quarterly provides
news, analysis, reviews and humor
aimed at ridding the world of bigots,
bosses and patriarchs with special
attention to the issues and leadership of women, people of color and
sexual minoritites.

FRONTIERS NEWS MAGAZINE

P.O. Box 46367
West Hollywood, CA 90046
(213) 848-2222
Fax: (213) 656-8784
webmaster@frontiersweb.com
www.frontiersweb.com

A comprehensive magazine for and
about lesbian/gay issues and rights.

FUNDING EXCHANGE

Newsletter of the Paul Robeson
Fund for Independent Media
666 Broadway #500
New York, NY 10012
(212) 529-5300
Fax: (212) 982-9272
fexexc@aol.com
www.fex.org

This newsletter of Funding
Exchange, a network of fifteen community foundations throughout the
United States, reports on community-based efforts to address a wide
range of social problems.

FUNNY TIMES

P.O. Box 18530
Cleveland Heights, OH 44118
(216) 371-8600
Fax: (216) 371-8696
ft@funnytimes.com
www.funnytimes.com

Now in its twelfth year, *Funny Times*
collects the best of the best in the
cartoon and humor world. Humor
enthusiasts enjoy the monthly dose
of thought-provoking cartoons and
funny stories about everyday life and
politics. "Our humor is poignant but
not mean-spirited, sexist or boring—
though our politics annoy most
Republicans," say its editors.

FUSE MAGAZINE

401 Richmond St.W, Suite 454
Toronto, ON
Canada
(416) 340-8026
Fax: (416) 340-0494
fuse@interlog.com
www.fusemagazine.org

Blending critical analysis of contemporary art, curatorship and social/political events related to art practices in diverse cultural and racial communities, *Fuse* focuses on cultural politics and explorations of the relationship between art and social changes.

GAUNTLET

309 Powell Rd.
Springfield, PA 19064
(610) 328-5476
Fax: (610) 328-9949
info@gauntletpress.com
www.gauntletpress.com

A magazine devoted to exploring the limits of free speech.

GENEWATCH

Published by the Council for Responsible Genetics
5 Upland Road Suite #3
Cambridge, MA 02140
(617) 868-0870
Fax: (617) 491-5344
crg@gene-watch.org
www.gene-watch.org

This publication provides a forum for discussing, evaluating and distributing information and opinions about the social and environmental aspects of genetic engineering.

GEO NEWSLETTER

Grassrooots Economic Organizing
177 Kiles Rd.
Stillwater, PA 17878
(570) 784-7384
editors@geonewsletter.org
www.geonewsletter.org

GEO (Grassroots Economic Organizing) Newsletter is a bimonthly publication that reports on worker co-operatives and community-based economies around the globe, and their development through local co-operative action. *GEO* is a global forum for the co-operative movement.

GLAADNOTES

150 West 26th Street, Suite 503
New York, NY 10001
(800) GAY-MEDIA
Fax: (212) 629-3225
glaad@glaad.org
www.glaad.org

This quarterly newsletter promotes fair, accurate, inclusive media representation of lesbian, gay, bisexual and transgendered people.

GLOBAL INFORMATION NETWORK

146 West 29th St. #7E
New York, NY 10001
(212) 244-3123
Fax: (212) 244-3522
ipsgin@igc.org
www.globalinfo.org

Global Information Network, a not-for-profit news and world media operation, is the largest distributor of Developing World news services—including the award-winning Inter Press Service—in the United States.

GLOBAL OUTLOOK

R R 2, Shanty Bay
Ontario, Canada L0L 2L0
Editor@globalresearch.ca
www.globalresearch.ca

Global Outlook is the publication of the Center for Research on Globalisation (CRG), an independent research and media group of progressive writers, scholars and activists committed to curbing the tide of "globalization" and "disarming" the New World Order.

GLOBAL PESTICIDE CAMPAIGNER

49 Powell St., Suite 500
San Francisco, CA 94102
(415) 981-1771
Fax: (415) 981-1991
panna@panna.org
www.igc.org/panna/resources/gpc.html

Providing environmental, health, and other information about pesticides, ecological pest control and sustainable agriculture, *GPC* is published by Pesticide Action Network.

GNOSIS MAGAZINE

P.O. Box 14820
San Francisco, CA 94114
(415) 974-0600
Fax: (415) 974-0366
gnosis@well.com
www.lumen.org

A publication devoted to the exploration of spiritual and esoteric paths of Western Civilization.

GOVERNMENT INFORMATION INSIDER

1742 Connecticut Ave. NW
Washington, DC 20009
(202) 234-8494
Fax: (202) 234-8584
www.ombwatch.org

A magazine published by OMB (White House Office of Management and Budget) Watch that focuses on government secrecy and the public's right to know.

GRASSROOTS FUNDRAISING JOURNAL

3781 Broadway
Oakland, CA 94611
(510) 596-8160
Fax: (510) 596-8822
chardon@chardonpress.com
www.chardonpress.com

Grassroots Fundraising Journal, published by Chardon Press, is a how-to magazine providing information on all aspects of fundraising for groups working for social change.

GREAT IDEAS IN EDUCATION

P.O. Box 328
Brandon, VT 05733-0328
(800) 639-4122
Fax: (802) 247-8312
info@great-ideas.org
www.great-ideas.org

Great Ideas In Education is a guide to holistic education.

GUILD NOTES

126 University Place, 5th Floor
New York, NY 10003
(212) 627-2656
Fax: (212) 627-2404
nlgno@nlg.org
www.nlg.org

Guild Notes is a newsletter of the National Lawyers Guild.

HA!

P.O. Box 1282
Carrboro, NC 27510
gmonster@email.unc.edu
www.ibiblio.org/hazine

Brought to you by the Lilith Collective, *HA!* is a venue for women's voices and self-expression, as well as a forum for feminist issues. We recognize the diversity of women and therefore the existence of multiple feminisms.

HAITI PROGRES

1398 Flatbush Ave.
Brooklyn, NY 11210
(718) 434-5551
editor@haiti-progres.com
www.haiti-progres.com

An English, French and Creole Haitian weekly.

HARDBOILED

201 Heller Lounge, UC Berkeley
Berkeley, CA 94720-4500
hardboiled@uclink4.berkeley.edu
www.hardboiled.org

You will find in these pages coverage of everything from underground films and music to education reform; profiles of community leaders to exposes of police brutality against

Asian-Americans; deconstructions of Asian pornography to a look into the world of Asian-American 'zines and independent media

HEALTH LETTER

5 Thomas Circle, Suite 500
Washington, DC 20005
(202) 483-1652
Fax: (202) 483-7369
www.citizens.org

Health Letter provides critical information on health care issues.

HEALTH QUEST: TOTAL WELLNESS FOR BODY, MIND AND SPIRIT

200 Highpoint Dr., Suite 215
Chalfont, PA 18914
(215) 822-7935
Fax: (215) 997-9582
shart@healthquestmag.com
www.healthquestmag.com

This national quarterly focuses specifically on health and wellness in the African-American community. It is a guide to total wellness: mental, spiritual, emotional and physical. Taking a holistic approach, *Health Quest* addresses traditional health concerns such as diet, nutrition, exercise and disease, while probing broader health-impacting issues like environment, alternative forms of healing and much more.

HEART & SOUL

315 Park Ave. S, 11th Floor
New York, NY 10010
(646) 654-4200
Fax: (646) 654-4244
www.heartandsoul.com

This national, bimonthly publication addresses the total well-being of body, mind and spirit of African-American women.

HERMENAUT

179 Boylston St.
Jamaica Plains, MA 02130
(617) 522-7100
info@hermenaut.com
www.hermenaut.com

An irregularly published journal of philosophy and pop culture, Hermenaut has been variously described as "a 'zine that gives voice to indie intellectual thought," "a scholarly journal minus the university," and "a sounding board for thinking folk who operate outside the ivory tower." Founded in 1992 by a rag-tag group of outsider intellectuals, *Hermenaut* uses the tools of philosophy, sociology and critical theory to explode the received notions of academia and the hipster demimonde alike.

HIGH COUNTRY NEWS

P.O. Box 1090
Paonia, CO 81428
(800) 905-1155
editor@hcn.org
www.hcn.org

High Country News is a nonprofit, biweekly newspaper reporting on public lands and rural communities in the western U.S. to over 21,000 subscribers. It is a respected independent source for environmental news, analysis and commentary.

HIGH GRADER MAGAZINE

P.O. BOX 714
Colbalt, ON P0J 1C0
Canada
(705) 679-5533
Fax: (705) 679-5234
highgrade@nt.net
www.grievousangels.com/highgrader

News reporting and offbeat cultural comments from a working-class perspective.

HIGHTOWER LOWDOWN, THE

P.O. Box 20596
New York, NY 10011
(212) 741-2365
Fax: (212) 979-2055
info@jimhightower.com
www.Jimhightower.com

A twice-monthly populist newsletter featuring Jim Hightower.

HINDUISM TODAY

Kauai's Hindu Monastery
Kapaa, HI 96746-9304
(808) 822-7032 x230
Fax: (808) 822-4351
letters@hindu.org
www.hinduismtoday.com

Hinduism Today is a magazine to foster Hindu solidarity.

HIP MAMA

P.O. Box 12525
Portland, OR 97212
info@hipmama.com
www.hipmama.com

Covering the culture and politics of parenting, *Hip Mama:The Parenting 'Zine* is a publication for progressive families.

HISPANIC ENGINEER

Career Communications Group, Inc.
729 East Pratt St., Suite 504
Baltimore, MD 21202
(410) 244-7101
Fax: (410) 752-1837
www.ccgmag.com or www.black-engineer.com

This nationally distributed quarterly is dedicated to promoting opportunities for Hispanic Americans in science and technology.

HUMAN RIGHTS TRIBUNE
8 York St., Suite 302
Ottawa, ON K1N 5S6
Canada
(613) 789-7407
Fax: (613) 789-7414
hri@hri.ca
www.hri.ca

Published quarterly, *Human Rights Tribune* also has a Web edition, Human Rights Internet, that features links to human rights Web sites, job postings from human rights organizations and databases.

HUMANIST, THE
Journal of the American Humanist Association
1777 T Street NW
Washington, DC 20009-9088
(202) 238-9088 and (866) 486-2647
Fax: (202) 238-9003
AHA@erols.com
humanist.net/publications/humanist.html

The Humanist is a magazine of critical inquiry and social concern.

HUMANIST IN CANADA
P.O. Box 3769, Station C
Ottawa, ON K1V 4J8
(613) 749-8929
Fax: (613) 749-8929
jepiercy@cyberus.ca
www.humanists.net/hic

Published by Canadian Humanist Publications Inc. for nonbelievers interested in social issues, *Humanist In Canada* explores contemporary issues from a humanistic viewpoint committed to free inquiry in a pluralistic, democratic society.

IDS INSIGHTS
177 East 87th Street, Suite 501
New York, NY 10128
(212) 423-9237
Fax: (212) 423-9352
IDSInsights@institutefordemocracy.org
www.idsonline.org

IMAGES
Gay & Lesbian Alliance Against Defamation
150 West 26th St.reet, Suite 503
New York, NY 10001
(800) GAY-MEDIA
Fax: (617) 426-3594
images@glaad.org
www.glaad.org

A biannual journal, *Images* brings together the voices of academic researchers, activists, artists, journalists and other media professionals to explore the ways media shape lesbian, gay, bisexual and transgender lives.

IMPACT PRESS
PMB 361, 10151 University Blvd
Orlando, FL 32817
(407) 263-5504
editor@impactpress.com
www.impactpress.com

Impact Press is a nonprofit,
bimonthly, socio-political magazine
that features aggressive journalism,
biting commentary and a healthy
dose of satire: covering issues the
way the media should.

IN THE FAMILY
P.O. Box 5387
Takoma Park, MD 20913
(301) 270-4771
Fax: (301) 270-4660
LMarkowitz@aol.com
www.inthefamily.com

In the Family is the only magazine
that focuses exclusively on lesbian,
gay, bisexual and transgender families, posing challenging questions
and drawing on the wisdom of mental health experts who have been
offering concrete advice and creative solutions to les-bi-gay families
for years.

IN THESE TIMES
2040 N Milwaukee Ave., 2nd Floor
Chicago, IL 60647-4002
(773) 772-0100
Fax: (773) 772-4180

itt@inthesetimes.com
www.inthesetimes.com

In These Times provides independent news and views you won't find
anywhere else.

INDEPENDENT REVIEW, THE
100 Swan Way
Oakland, CA 94621-1428
(800) 927-8733
Fax: (510) 568-6040
info@independent.org
www.independent.org

Published by the Independent
Institute, the *Independent Review* is
a journal of political economy.

INDIA CURRENTS
P.O. Box 21285
San Jose, CA 95151
(408) 274-6966
Fax: (408) 274-2733
publisher@indiacurrents.com
www.Indiacurrents.com

India Currents magazine is one
important facet of America's emerging multicultural identity: a monthly publication devoted to the exploration of the arts and culture of
India as it exists in the United
States.

INDIA JOURNAL

15605 S. Carenita Road, Suite. 107
Santa Fe Springs, CA 90670-5648
(562) 802-9720
Fax: (562) 802-9750
info@indiajournal.com
www.indiajournal.com

The leading weekly Indo-American newspaper in Southern California, *India Journal* is the oldest and most reliable publication for information on the Indo-American community.

INDIA WEST

933 Mac Arthur Blvd.
San Leandro, CA 94577-3062
(510) 383-1140
Fax: (510) 383-1155
info@indiawest.com
www.indiawest.com

India West, a publication indispensable to the Indo-American community and those interested in South Asian affairs, celebrated its twenty-fifth anniversary in 2001.

INDIA WORLDWIDE

244 5th Avenue.
New York, NY 10001
(877) 481-0395
subscription@newsindia-times.com
www.newsIndia-times.com

A monthly publication for and about people of Indian descent.

INDIAN COUNTRY TODAY (LAKOTA TIMES)

P.O. Box 4250
Rapid City, SD 57709
(605) 341-0011
Fax: (605) 341-6940
editor@indiancountry.com
www.indiancountry.com

Published weekly with distribution in all 50 states and 15 foreign countries, *Indian Country Today* is the most influential and widely read Native American newspaper in the United States. Its regional section covers Pine Ridge Reservation.

INDUSTRIAL WORKER

P.O. Box 13476
Philadelphia, PA 19101-3476
(313) 483-3548
Fax: (313) 483-4050
iw@iww.org
www.iww.org

The *Industrial Worker* is the monthly newspaper of the Industrial Workers of the World, or Wobblies. Every issue contains news of the world labor struggles and analysis of the labor movement and economy from a Wobbly perspective.

INROADS

3777 Kent Ave.
Montreal, QC K3S 1N4
Canada (514) 731-2691
Fax: (514) 731-8256
inroads@canada.com
qsilver.queensu.ca/~inroads

A literary annual in which knowledgeable Canadians with different viewpoints address political, social and economic issues.

INSIDE TRANSPORTATION

888 16th Street NW, Suite 650
Washington, DC 20006
(202) 628-9262
Fax: (202) 628-0391
ttd@ttd.org
www.ttd.org

Inside Transportation is the official publication of the Transportation Trades Department of the AFL-CIO.

INSURGENT, THE

Erb Memorial Union, Suite 1
Eugene, OR 97403-1228
(541) 346-3716
collective@theinsurgent.org
www.theinsurgent.org

The Insurgent seeks to provide a forum for those working towards a society free from oppression.

INTELLIGENCE REPORT

Journal of the Southern Poverty Law
Center
400 Washington Ave.
Montgomery, AL 36104
(334) 264-0286
Fax: (334) 956-8485
www.splcenter.org

A quarterly journal offering in-depth analysis of political extremism and bias crimes in the United States, *Intelligence Report* profiles far right leaders, monitors domestic terrorism and reports on the activities of extremist groups.

INTERNATIONAL EXAMINER

622 S. Washington St.
Seattle, WA 98104
(206) 624-3925
Fax: (206) 624-3046
editorial@xaminer.com

Published since 1974, the *International Examiner* is the oldest English-language Asian community newspaper. It features Pacific Rim and national news and presents exclusive stories on Asian-Americans.

INTERNATIONAL JOURNAL OF HEALTH SERVICES

Baywood Publishing
P.O. Box 337
Amityville, NY 11701
(631) 691-1270
Fax: (631) 691-1770
info@baywood.com
www.baywood.com/search/PreviewJournal.asp?qsRecord=6

The *International Journal of Health Services* covers social policy, political economy, sociology, history, philosophy, ethics and law in relation to health and health care.

IRE JOURNAL, THE

Missouri School of Journalism,
138 Neff Annex
Columbia, MO 65211
(573) 882-2042
Fax: (573) 882-5431
info@ire.org
www.ire.org

The *IRE Journal* is published six times a year by IRE (Investigative Reporters and Editors, Inc.) and contains journalist profiles, how-to stories, reviews, investigative ideas and backgrounding tips. The Journal also provides members with the latest news on upcoming events, training and employment opportunities in the field of journalism.

IRISH AMERICA

432 Park Ave. S, Suite #1503
New York, NY 10016
(212) 725-2993
Fax: (212) 779-1198
Irishamag@aol.com
www.irishamerica.com

Published bimonthly, *Irish America*, the only national four-color Irish magazine in the United States, is published for those Americans who seek a better understanding of the Irish in the U.S.

IRISH VOICE

432 Park Avenue S, Suite 1503
New York, NY 10016
(212) 684-3366
Fax: (212) 779-1198
editorial@irishvoice.com
www.irishvoice.com

Irish Voice is a weekly, national newspaper providing news and information to the Irish and Irish-American community in the U.S. The paper focuses on local and international issues including politics, sports, entertainment and local events.

IRONWORKER
1750 New York Ave. NW, Suite 700
Washington, DC 20006
(202) 383-4800
Fax: (202) 638-4856
webmaster@ironworker.com
www.ironworker.com

The newsletter of the Iron
Workers Union.

ISSUES IN SCIENCE AND TECHNOLOGY
Cecil and Ida Green Center for the
Study of Science and Society
University of Texas at Dallas,
P.O. Box 830688
Richardson, TX 75083-0688
(972) 883-6325
Fax: (972) 883-6327
kfinnera@nas.edu
www.nas.edu

This National Academy of
Sciences quarterly features articles that analyze current topics in
science, technology and health
policy and recommend actions by
government, industry, academia
and individuals to solve pressing
problems.

IUE NEWS
1275 K Street, Suite #600
Washington, DC 20005
(202) 513-6300
Fax: (202) 785-4563

info@iue.org
www.iue.org

The official publication of the
International Union of Elecronic,
Electrical, Salaried, Machine and
Furniture Workers, AFL-CIO.

JEWISH WEEK, THE
1501 Broadway, Suite 505
New York, NY 10036
(212) 921-7822
Fax: (212)921-8420
info@jewishweek.com
www.thejewishweek.com

This national weekly seeks to build
and strengthen Jewish community
while championing an aggressive
and independent press. *The Jewish
Week* is supportive of, but not
beholden to, the organized Jewish
community. Its first loyalty is to the
truth.

JFL (JOURNAL FOR LIVING), THE
22 Elm St.
Albany, NY 12202
(518) 462-5814
jflmag@aol.com
www.jflmag.com

This journal makes available the
tools for transforming individual
lives and ultimately the entire community.

JOURNAL OF BLACKS IN HIGHER EDUCATION, THE
200 West 57th Street, 15th Floor
New York, NY 10019
(212) 399-1084
Fax: (212) 245-1973
info@jbhe.com
www.jbhe.com

The striking new importance of higher education in the lives of black Americans sparked the introduction of this quarterly journal. Now, as never before, African Americans need new information about the governance, policies and practices of our colleges and universities.

JOURNAL OF COMMUNITY PRACTICE
University of North Carolina
School of Social Work, CB #3550
Chapel Hill, NC 27599
(919) 962-1225
Fax: (919) 962-0890
ssw@unc.edu
www.ssw.unc.edu/sowoso/
journals_index.htm

A journal of organizing, planning, development and change.

JOURNAL OF PESTICIDE REFORM
P.O. Box 1393
Eugene, OR 97440
(541) 344-5044
Fax: (541) 344-6923
info@pesticide.org
www.efn.org/~ncap

Published by the Northwest Coalition for Alternatives to Pesticides (NCAP), the Journal of Pesticide Reform is a quarterly dedicated to sustainable resource management, prevention of pest problems, use of alternatives to pesticides and the right to be free from pesticide exposure.

JOURNAL OF PRISONERS ON PRISONS
P.O. Box 70068 Place Bell R.P.O.
Ottawa, ON K2P 2M3
Canada
(613) 562-5800 x1796
jpp@jpp.org
www.jpp.org/

JPP is an independent, academic journal that publishes the analyses and commentary of prisoners and former prisoners on contemporary criminal justice issues.

JOURNALISM AND MASS COMMUNICATION QUARTERLY
National Center for
Communication Studies,
George Washington University
Washington, DC 20052
(202) 994-6226
Fax: (202) 994-5806

aejmc@sc.edu

commfaculty.fullerton.edu/lester/ot
herwork/aejmc/pubs.html#jmcq
Published by the Association for
Education in Journalism and Mass
Communication, this scientific
research publication examines journalism and mass communication.

KONFORMIST, THE

P.O. Box 24825
Los Angeles, CA 90024-0825
(310) 737-1081
Fax: (310) 737-1081
robalini@aol.com
www.konformist.com

The Konformist promotes media
activism and has an Internet magazine dedicated to "rebellion, con-
spiracy and subversion."

KOREA TIMES

4525 Wilshire Blvd.
Los Angeles, CA 90010
(213) 692-2043
Fax: (213) 738-1103
www.korealink.co.kr

Korea Times is a monthly bilingual
family journal for parents and their
children, with a specific focus on
Korean families living in the United
States.

LA OFERTA REVIEW INC.

1376 North 4th Street
San Jose, CA 95112
(408) 436-7850
Fax: (408) 436-7861
laoferta@bayarea.net
www.laoferta.com

The most awarded bilingual newspaper in the United States.

LABOR NEWS FOR WORKING FAMILIES

2521 Channing Way, #5555
Berkeley, CA 94720
(510) 643-7088
Fax: (510) 642-6432
lpws@home.iir.berkeley.edu
laborproject.berkeley.edu

Labor News For Working Families
highlights union policies and bene-
fits, including family leave, child
care, elder care and flexible work.

LABOR NOTES

7435 Michigan Ave.
Detroit, MI 48210
(313) 842-6262
Fax: (313) 842-0227
labornotes@labornotes.org
www.labornotes.org

Aimed at rebuilding the labor movement through democracy and member activity, *Labor Notes* offers
news and information for workplace
activists.

LABORATORY MEDICINE
2100 W Harrison St.
Chicago, IL 60612
(312) 738-1336
Fax: (312) 738-0101
info@ascp.org
www.ascp.org

Laboratory Medicine, a publication of the American Society of Clinical Pathologists, is a not-for-profit medical society organized exclusively for educational, scientific and charitable purposes.

LAMBDA BOOK REVIEW/ JAMES WHITE REVIEW
P.O. Box 73910
Washington, DC 20056-3910
(202) 682-0952
Fax: (202) 682-0955
jane@lambdalit.org

Published by the Lambda Literary Foundation, these review magazines cover trade news and publishing information for gay and lesbian writers.

LATIN AMERICAN PERSPECTIVES
UC Riverside, Department of Economics
1150 University, Suite 107
Riverside, CA 92521
(909) 787-5037 x1571
Fax: (909) 787-5685
chilcote@mail.ucr.edu
www.ucr.edu

Latin American Perspectives is an academic journal on Latin American issues.

LEFT BUSINESS OBSERVER
P.O. Box 953
New York, NY 10014-0704
(212) 874-4020
Fax: (212) 874-3137
dhenwood@panix.com
www.panix.com/~dhenwood/LBO_home.html

A monthly newsletter on economics and politics in the U.S. and around the world.

LEFT CURVE
P.O. Box 472
Oakland, CA 94604-0472
(510) 763-7193
leftcurv@wco.com
www.ncal.verio.com/~leftcurv

Left Curve is an artist-produced magazine addressing cultural forms as they relate to the problems of modernity. It recognizes the destructiveness of commodity systems to all life.

LEGAL TIMES
153 Kearny St.
San Francisco, CA 94108
(800) 903-9872
Fax: (415) 352-5287
legaltimes@legaltimes.com
www.law.com/dc

A weekly legal newspaper.

LIBERTY
P.O. Box 1181
Port Townsend, WA 98368
(800) 854-6991
www.rahul.net/liberty/liberty

A review of thought, culture and politics.

LIBRARIANS AT LIBERTY
1716 SW Williston Rd.
Gainesville, FL 32608
(352) 335-2200
willett@fdt.net
www.LibLib.com

Librarians at Liberty, published by CRISES Press, aims to give those working in libraries and related fields an unconstrained opportunity to express professional concerns.

LILIPOH
P.O. Box 649
Nyack, NY 10960
(845) 268-2627
Fax: (845) 268-2764

lilipoh@aol.com
www.lilipoh.com

LILIPOH (Life, Liberty, and the Pursuit of Happiness) is a unique wellness quarterly dedicated to informed choice in healthcare.

LILITH
250 West 57th Street
New York, NY 10107
(212) 757-0818
Fax: (212) 757-5705
LilithMag@aol.com
www.lilith.org

Lilith is a full color magazine for Jewish women. It encourages women's participation in Jewish life and counters the negative stereotypes that sometimes cause Jewish women to shun their Jewish identity.

LINGUAFRANCA
135 Madison Avenue
New York, NY 10016
(212) 684-9884
Fax: (212) 684-9879
edit@linguafranca.com
www.linguafranca.com

With its fiercely independent reportage turning controversy into interesting journalism, *Linguafranca: The Review of Academic Life* is the connection to the ivory tower.

LITTLE INDIA

1800 Oak Lane
Reading, PA 19604
(610) 396-0366
Fax: (610) 396-0367
littleindia@aol.com
www.littleindia.com

Little India is a monthly feature magazine devoted exclusively to overseas Indian life. The magazine, currently in its sixth year of publishing, has an editorial focus on the nearly one million Indians in the United States. Every month the magazine brings its readers trenchant commentaries on overseas Indian life and the works and visions of overseas Indian artists, performers and professionals.

LRA'S ECONOMIC NOTES

330 West 42nd Street, 13th floor
New York, NY 10001
(212) 714-1677
Fax: (212) 714-1674
info@laborresearch.org
www.laborresearch.org

LRA's Economic Notes offers views on labor, economics and politics for labor policy makers.

MASALA

276 5th Avenue, Suite 603
New York, NY 10001
(212) 627-2522
Fax: (212) 685-7255
webmaster@masala.com
www.masala.com

This quarterly publication covers issues of interest to Asians and Pacific Islanders.

MAVIN MAGAZINE

600 1st Avenue, Suite 501
Seattle, WA 98104-2229
(206) 622-7101
Fax: (206) 622-2231
matt@mavinfoundation.org
www.mavinmag.com

Mavin is an internationally distributed print and online magazine that celebrates the mixed race experience. Started in 1998 on the campus of Wesleyan University, Mavin recognizes that mixed-race and transracially adopted people represent every community. The word mavin has roots in Hebrew and means "one who understands."

MEDIA BYPASS

4900 Tippecanoe Dr.
Evansville, IN 47715
(812) 477-8670
Fax: (812) 477-8677
subscribe@4bypass.com

www.mediabypass.com

A national magazine from alternative sources providing unsuppressed national news for concerned Americans.

MEDIA CONSORTIUM, THE
1355 North Highway Dr.
Fenton, St. Louis County, MO 63099
(800) 325-3338
Fax: (636) 827-6761
postmaster@delve.com
207.239.118.26/delvemain.asp

An independent, investigative news company with the goal of generating original journalism through a variety of media outlets.

MEDIA WATCH
P.O. Box 618
Santa Cruz, CA 95061-0618
(800) 631-6355
Fax: (408) 423-6355
mwatch@cruzio.com
www.mediawatch.com

Media Watch works to challenge media bias through education and action.

MIDDLE EAST REPORT
1500 Massachusetts Ave. NW, Suite 119
Washington, DC 20005
(202) 223-3677

Fax: (202) 223-3604
ctoensing@merip.org
www.merip.org

Offering an independent critical voice on the Middle East, *Middle East Report* welcomes and will pay for current photographs of the region.

MILITARY AND THE ENVIRONMENT
222-B View St.
Mountain View, CA 94041
(415) 904-7751
Fax: (415) 904-7765
cpro@igc.apc.org
www.igc.org

Published by the Pacific Studies Center, *Military and the Environment* is a citizen's report newsletter aimed at educating the public about current issues and legislation related to the military and its impact on the environment.

MIND FREEDOM JOURNAL
Formerly Dendron Magazine
P.O. Box 11284
Eugene, OR 97440-3484
(541) 345-9106
Fax: (541) 345-3737
office@mindfreedom.org

Mind Freedon Journal is a publication of the Support Coalition International, an alliance of almost one hundred grassroots groups in thirteen countries united to win human rights in the mental health system.

MINORITY BUSINESS ENTREPRENEUR (MBE)
3528 Torrance Blvd., Suite 101
Torrance, CA 90503-4803
(310) 540-9398
Fax: (310) 792-8263
gconrad@mbemag.com
www.mbemag.com

A multi-ethnic, bimonthly business magazine.

MONTHLY REVIEW
122 West 27th Street
New York, NY 10001
(212) 691-2555
Fax: (212) 727-3676
promo@monthlyreview.org
www.monthlyreview.org

An independent socialist magazine, *MR* offers a unique blend of scholarship and activism, critical understanding and accessibility.

MOTHER JONES
731 Market St., 6th floor
San Francisco, CA 94103
(415) 665-6637 and (800) 438-6656
Fax: (415) 665-6696
subscribe@motherjones.com
www.motherjones.com

This magazine of investigative journalism now has an online sister publication, mojowire.

MOTHERING
P.O. Box 1690
Santa Fe, NM 87505
(505) 984-8116
Fax: (505) 986-8335
Info@mothering.com
www.mothering.com

Mothering celebrates the experience of parenthood as worthy of one's best efforts, and fosters awareness of the immense importance and value of parenthood and family life in the deveopment of the full human potential of parents and children. Recognizing parents as the experts, *Mothering* provides truly helpful information with which parents can make informed choices.

MOUNTAIN ASTROLOGER
P.O. Box 970
Cedar Ridge, CA 95924
(800) 287-4828
Fax: (530) 477-9423
subs@mountainastrologer.com
www.mountainastrologer.com

The Mountain Astrologer is widely acknowledged as the best English-language astrology magazine in the world today.

MOUNTAINFREAK

P.O. Box 4149
Telluride, CO 81435
(970) 728-9731
Fax: (970) 728.9821
freaks@mountainfreak.com
www.mountainfreak.com

An environmental magazine focusing on mountains and mountain recreation in the United States.

MOUTH: VOICE OF THE DISABILITY NATION

61 Brighton St.
Rochester, NY 14607-2656
(716) 244-6599
Fax: (716) 244-9798
www.mouthmag.com/index.htm

Mouth speaks the unspeakable, questions the unquestionable, follows the money in the $100 billion disability exploitation industry. News and activism: no tragedy; no bravery; no ads.

MOXIE

1230 Glen Ave.
Berkeley, CA 94708
(510) 540-5510
emily@moxiemag.com
www.moxiemag.com

Moxie inspires women to live boldly, pursue adventures, take risks and provide others with vibrant role models in the process.

MS. MAGAZINE

20 Exchange Place, 22nd floor
New York, NY 10005
(212) 509-2092
Fax: (212) 509-2407
info@msmagazine.com
www.msmagazine.com

This founding magazine of the feminist movement is ad-free, with a national and international focus on issues affecting women.

MSRRT NEWSLETTER: LIBRARY ALTERNATIVES

4645 Columbus Ave. S
Minneapolis, MN 55407
(612) 694-8572
Fax: (612) 541-8600
edmiston@cs.unca.edu
www.cs.unca.edu/~edmiston/msrrt

Published by the Minnesota Library Association Social Responsibilities Round Table, this newsletter provides news, commentary and networking info for activist librarians and cultural workers, with reviews of alternative press publications and alternative media.

MULTINATIONAL MONITOR
P.O. Box 19405
Washington, DC 20036
(202) 387-8030
Fax: (202) 234-5176
monitor@essential.org
www.essential.org
multinationalmonitor.org

MM tracks corporate activity, especially in the Third World.

NABJ JOURNAL
8701 Adelphi Road
Adelphi, MD 20783-1716
(301) 445-7100
Fax: (301) 445-7101
nabj@nabj.org
nabj.org

Published ten times a year, the *NABJ Journal* is the publication of the National Association of Black Journalist, the largest media organization of people of color in the world.

NACLA REPORT ON THE AMERICAS
475 Riverside Dr., Suite 454
New York, NY 10115
(212) 870-3146
Fax: (212) 870-3305
nacla@nacla.org
www.nacla.org

NACLA, for thirty years, has been the best source for alternative information and analysis on Latin America, the Caribbean, and U.S. foreign policy in the region. *NACLA* analyzes the major political, social and economic trends in Latin America in an accessible format not found anywhere else.

NAJA NEWS
3359 36th Avenue South
Minneapolis, MN 55406
(612) 729-9244
Fax: (612) 729-9373
naja@naja.com
www.naja.com

The quarterly newsletter of the Native American Journalists' Association.

NATION, THE
33 Irving Place, 8th floor
New York, NY 10003
(212) 209-5400
Fax: (212) 982-9000
info@thenation.com
www.thenation.com

Founded in 1865, *The Nation* continues to be a leading forum for leftist debate and investigative journalism.

NATIONAL CAMPAIGN FOR FREEDOM OF EXPRESSION QUARTERLY

1429 G Street NW, PMB#416
Washington, DC 20005-2009
(202) 393-2787
Fax: (202) 347-7376
ncfe@ncfe.net
www.ncfe.net

This quarterly is an educational and advocacy magazine for artists, arts organizations, audience members and concerned citizens interested in protecting and extending freedom of artistic expression and fighting censorship throughout the U.S.

NATIONAL CATHOLIC REPORTER

115 East Armour Blvd
Kansas City, MO 64111
(816) 531-0538 and (800) 333-7373
Fax: (816) 968-2268
ncr_editor@natcath.com
www.natcath.com

An independent, Catholic newsweekly inspired by the second vatican, *National Catholic Reporter* has covered events related to the church for more than thirty years.

NATIONAL GREEN PAGES

A Publication of Co-op America
1612 K Street NW, Suite 600
Washington, DC 20006
(800) 58-GREEN and (202) 872-5307
Fax: (202) 331-8166
info@coopamerica.org
www.greenpages.org

This annual directory of thousands of responsible businesses, products, and services is a wonderful resource.

NATIVE AMERICAS-AKWE:KON'S JOURNAL OF INDIGENOUS ISSUES

450 Caldwell Hall, Cornell University
Ithaca, NY 14853
(607) 255-4308
Fax: (607) 255-0185
nativeamericas@cornell.edu
nativeamericas.aip.cornell.edu

This publication of the American Indian Program at Cornell University covers the most important and critical issues of concern to Native peoples throughout the western hemisphere, synthesizing the many voices, perspectives and information for and about indigenous aboriginal peoples.

NEA TODAY
1201 16th Street NW
Washington, DC 20036
(202) 833-4000
Fax: (202) 822-7206
NEAToday@aol.com
www.nea.org

This, the magazine of the National Education Association, provides insights on education challenges facing the U.S. today.

NEIGHBORHOOD WORKS, THE
2125 W North Ave.
Chicago, IL 60647
(773) 278-4800
Fax: (773) 278-3840
info@cnt.org
www.cnt.org

This bimonthly publication of the Center for Neighborhood Technology seeks out those people, projects and issues that demonstrate substantial principles at work in urban areas.

NETWORK JOURNAL, THE
139 Fulton St., Suite 407
New York, NY 10038
(212) 962-3791
Fax: (212) 962-3537
editors@trj.com
www.tnj.com

The Network Journal (TNJ) was founded with the recognition that an increasing number of people, many of whom are African-American professionals, are starting up their own businesses. TNJ offers ideas in the areas of management, marketing, finance, office technology, banking and taxes. The publication also carries listings of pertinent seminars, entertainment events and reviews.

NETWORK NEWS, THE
Journal of the The National Women's Health Network
514 10th Street NW
Washington, DC 20004
(202) 347-1140
Fax: (202) 347-1168
info@womenshealthnetwork.org
www.womenshealthnetwork.org

A biweekly newsletter focusing on women's health and related subjects.

NEW CITIZEN, THE
34 Wall Street, #407
Ashville, NC 28801
(704) 255-0182
Fax: (704) 254-2286
cml@main.nc.us
www.main.nc.us/cml

This publication of the Citizens for Media Literacy links media literacy with the concepts and practices of citizenship and provides media analysis and criticism.

NEW DEMOCRACY

P.O. Box 427
Boston, MA 02130
(617) 323-7213
newdem@aol.com
www.newdemocracyworld.org

New Democracy was founded to help people in their struggle against capitalism: that is, to shape the world with anti-capitalist values of solidarity, equality, and democracy.

NEW INTERNATIONALIST

P.O. Box 1143
Lewiston, NY 14092
(906) 946-0407
Fax: (906) 946-0410
magazines@indas.on.ca
www.oneworld.org

This international journal exists to report on the issues of inequality and world poverty; to focus attention on the unjust relationship between the powerful and the powerless in both rich and poor countries; and to debate the campaign for the radical changes necessary.

NEW MOON FOR GIRLS

P.O. Box 3620
Duluth, MN 55803-3620
(218) 728-5507
newmoon@newmoon.org
www.newmoon.org/index.html

A magazine for every girl who wants her voice heard and her dreams taken seriously, and for every adult who cares about girls.

NEW PARTY NEWS

88 3rd Avenue, Suite 313
Brooklyn, NY 11217
(800) 200-1294
Fax: (718) 246-3718
newparty@newparty.org
www.newparty.org

This is the publication of the New Party, a grassroots-based democratic political party now in active formation in a dozen states.

NEW PERSPECTIVES QUARTERLY

10951 West Pico Blvd., 3rd Floor
Los Angeles, CA 90064
(310) 474-0011
npq@pacificnet.net
www.npq.org

This quarterly offers economic and political thought on a global scale, from different points of view in a thematic format.

NEW POLITICS

328 Clinton St.
Brooklyn, NY 11231
(718) 237-2048
newpol@igc.org
www.wpunj.edu/~newpol/default.htm

A journal of socialist thought, *New Politics* insists on the centrality of democracy to socialism and on the need to rely on mass movements from below for progressive social transformation.

NEW REPUBLIC, THE
1331 H Street NW, Suite 700
Washington, DC 20005
(202) 508-4444
Fax: (202) 331-0275
tnr@aol.com
www.thenewrepublic.com

America's leading weekly journal of political opinion.

NEW SCIENTIST
201 Spear St., Suite 400
San Francisco, CA 94105
(888) 800-8077
Fax: (800) 327-9021
ns.subs@qss-uk.com
www.newscientist.com

New Scientist is an English journal devoted to science and technology and their impact on the way we live.

NEW SOCIALIST
P.O. Box 167
Toronto, ON M5T 1R5
Canada
(416) 969-3209
newsoc@web.net
www.newsocialist.org

A journal that rejects bureaucratic

and authoritarian visions of socialism and looks instead to the radical tradition of socialism from below, *New Socialist* hopes to contribute to the building of a wider socialist movement in Canada and internationally.

NEW UNIONIST
2309 Nicollette Ave., Suite 102
Minneapolis, MN 55408
(651) 646-5546
nup@minn.net
www1.minn.net/~nup

This monthly paper is dedicated to building a rank-and-file working-class movement for fundamental social change to replace the present competitive, class-divided system of capitalism with the co-operative industrial community of economic democracy.

NEW YORK AMSTERDAM NEWS
2340 Frederick Douglass Blvd
New York, NY 10027
(212) 932-7400
Fax: (212) 222-3842

With a long and respected history and influential coverage of local, national and international topics, the *Amsterdam News,* provides a unique understanding of the New York community and the country. Publisher and Editor-in-Chief, Mr. Wilbert Tatum brings a world view to the paper.

NEWS FROM INDIAN COUNTRY

7831 N Grindstone Ave.
Hayward, WI 54843-2052
(715) 634-5226
Fax: (715) 634-3243
newsfic.aol.com
www.indiancountrynews.com

NFIC provides national native news and information, as well as cultural and pow wow updates.

NEWS INDIA TIMES

244 5th Avenue, Suite 400
New York, NY 10001
(877) 481-0395
subscription@news-india.com
www.newsindia-times.com

The weekly combines hard news from India and the U.S. concerning the community at large with features and columns of interest to women and children. *News India Times* is the only four-color English language weekly serving the million-strong Asian Indians settled in the United States.

NEWS MEDIA AND THE LAW

1815 N Fort Meyer Dr., Suite 900
Arlington, VA 22209
(800) 336-4243
Fax: (703) 807-2109
rcfp@rcfp.org
www.rcfp.org

This journal of the Reporter's Committee for Freedom of the Press is published quarterly and explores issues related to news reporting and the media, and the legal issues therein.

NEWS MEDIA UPDATE

1815 N Fort Meyer Dr., Suite 900
Arlington, VA 22209
(800) 336-4243
Fax: (703) 807-2109
rcfp@rcfp.org
www.rcfp.org

This twice-monthly newsletter of the Reporter's Committee for Freedom of the Press covers current media issues.

NEWS ON EARTH

541 West 25th Street, PMB 2245
New York, NY 10011
(212) 741-2365
Fax: (212) 979-2055
earthchanges@earthlink.net
www.earthchangestv.com

A politically independent newsletter that reports on the vital issues of the day and tells the real story of what is going on in Washington.

NEWSLETTER ON INTELLECTUAL FREEDOM
American Library Association
50 E Huron St.
Chicago, IL 60611
(800) 545-2433
Fax: (312) 280-4227
jkrug@ala.org
www.ala.org/alaorg/oif/nif_inf.html

This is the newsletter of the ALA's Office of Intellectual Freedom.

NEWSPAPER GUILD, THE
501 3rd Street NW, Suite 205
Washington, DC 20001
(202) 434-7177
Fax: (202) 434-1472
guild@cwa-union.org
www.newsguild.org

This newsletter of the Newspaper Guild services the Communications Workers of America's 30,000 members in the U.S. and Canada.

NEWSPAPER RESEARCH JOURNAL
Ohio University
Park Place & Court St.
Athens, OH 45701-2979
(740) 593-2590
Fax: (740) 593-2592
info@scrippsjschool.org
www.scripps.ohiou.edu

Produced by the Scripps Hall School of Journalism, this journal bridges the gap between the newspaper industry and academe.

NEWSPRINTS
P.O. Box 19405
Washington, DC 20036
(202) 387-8030
Fax: (202) 234-5176
newsprints@essential.org
www.essential.org/newsprints/news prints.html

Twice a month *Newsprints* publishes leads that the national dailies and network news shows miss: hard-hitting investigations and commentary by regional writers examining crucial concerns from more than 100 of the nation's highest circulating daily newspapers.

NEWSWATCH MONITOR
Newswatch Canada
c/o School of Communication
Simon Fraser University
8888 University Drive
Burnaby, BC
Canada
(604) 291-4905
Fax: (604) 291-3687
newswtch@sfu.ca
newswatch.cprost.sfu.ca

This quarterly newsletter of Newswatch Canada reports on Canada's media performance.

NEXUS
2940 E Colfax, #131
Denver, CO 80206
(303) 321-5006
Fax: (603) 754-4744
nexususa@earthlink.net
www.nexusmagazine.com

Nexus recognizes that humanity is undergoing a massive transformation and seeks to provide hard-to-find information so as to assist people through these changes. It is free of all religious, philosophical, political and organization affiliations.

NICHI BEI TIMES
P.O. Box 193098
San Francisco, CA 94119
(415) 921-6822
Fax: (415) 921-0770
nikkei@nichibeitimes.com
www.nichibeitimes.com

A Japanese-American news daily.

NLGJA
1420 K Street NW, Suite 910
Washington, DC 20005
(202) 588-9888
Fax: (202) 588-1818
info@nlgja.org
www.nlgja.org/alternatives/altindex.html

News and reports from the National Gay and Lesbian Journalists Association.

NOETIC SCIENCES REVIEW
101 San Antonio Rd.
Petaluma, CA 94952
(707) 779-8231
Fax: (707) 781-7420
nsreview@noetic.org
www.noetic.org

Published by the Institute for Noetic Sciences, *NSR* explores ways of transforming beliefs, values and actions in the world. Review articles are designed to engage, challenge and inspire both scientific and lay readers to expand perceptions of what is real and what is possible in our personal lives and in our communities. The magazine is sent to Institute members quarterly and is available at select newsstands.

NONVIOLENT ACTIVIST, THE
P.O. Box 30947
Philadelphia, PA 19104
(212) 228-0450
Fax: (212) 228-6193
nvweb@nonviolence.org
nonviolence.org

Political analysis from a pacifist perspective.

NORTHEASTERN ANARCHIST, THE
c/o Sabate Anarchist Collective
P.O. Box 230685
Boston, MA 02123
sabate36@juno.com
flag.blackened.net/nefac

The English-language magazine of the Northeastern Federation of Anarcho-Communists (NEFAC), the *Northeastern Anarchist* covers news of revolutionary resistance and publishes class struggle literature and anarchist theory, history and analysis.

NUCLEAR MONITOR, THE
1424 16th Street NW, Suite 404
Washington, DC 20036
(202) 328-0002
Fax: (202) 462-2183
hirsnet@hirs.org
www.nirs.org

This publication serves as a networking and advocacy center for citizens and groups concerned with nuclear power, radioactive waste and sustainable energy. *The Nuclear Monitor* is dedicated to a sound nonnuclear energy policy.

NUCLEAR RESISTER, THE
P.O. Box 43383
Tucson, AZ 85733-3383
(520) 323-8697
nukeresister@igc.org

www.nonviolence.org/nukeresister

NR provides information about and support for imprisoned anti-nuclear activists.

NUKEWATCH
The Progressive Foundation
P.O. Box 649
Luck, WI 54853
(715) 472-4185
Fax: (715) 472.4184
nukewtch@lakeland.ws
www.nukewatch.com

Nukewatch focuses on covering, investigating and exposing the nuclear industry.

NUTRITION ACTION HEALTHLETTER
Center for Science in the Public Interest
1875 Connecticut Ave. NW, Suite 300
Washington, DC 20009-5728
(202) 332-9110
Fax: (202) 265-4954
cspi@cspinet.org
www.cspinet.org

This publication of the Center for Science in the Public Interest is dedicated to promoting health and nutrition from a scientific, political and public interest perspective.

OBJECTOR, THE
630 20th Street, Suite #302
Oakland, CA 94612
(510) 465-1617
Fax: (510) 465-2459
info@objector.org
www.objector.org

This "magazine of conscience and resistance" is a publication of the Central Committee for Conscientious Objectors.

OFF OUR BACKS: A WOMEN'S NEWSJOURNAL
2337 B 18th Street NW
Washington, DC 20009
(202) 234-8072
Fax: (202) 234-8092
offourbacks@cs.com
www.igc.org/oob

A radical feminist newsjournal read all over the U.S. and in over fifty countries worldwide.

OKLAHOMA NATIVE AMERICAN TIMES
P.O. Box 692050
Tulsa, OK 74169
(918) 438-6548
Fax: (918) 438-6545
editor@okit.com
www.okit.com

A leading Indian news source for Oklahoma and the nation.

OMB WATCHER
1742 Connecticut Ave. NW
Washington, DC 20009-1171
(202) 234-8494
Fax: (202) 234-8584
ombwatch@ombwatch.org
www.ombwatch.org

This publication of OMB Watch focuses on budget issues, regulatory policy, nonprofit advocacy, access to government information and activities at the Office of Management and Budget in Washington.

ON EARTH
(Formerly the Amicus Journal)
40 West 20th Street
New York, NY 10011
(212) 727-4412
Fax: (212) 727-1773
OnEarth@nrdc.org
www.nrdc.org/OnEarth

This quarterly journal of thought and opinion on environmental issues is published by the National Resources Defense Council.

ON THE ISSUES
29-28 41st Avenue, 12th Floor
Long Island City, NY 11101-3303
(718) 459-9100
Fax: (718) 349-9458
ontheissues@compuserve.com
www.echonyc.com/~onissues

On The Issues: The Progressive

Woman's Quarterly is a feminist, humanist magazine of critical thinking designed to advance a deeper, more intelligent dialogue.

OTHER SIDE, THE

300 W Apsley
Philadelphia, PA 19144-4285
(215)849-2178
Fax: (215) 859-3755
editors@theotherside.org
www.theotherside.org

A socially progressive, bimonthly, ecumenical magazine, the Other Side since 1965 has advanced a healing Christian vision: a vision grounded in the redeeming ways of God.

OUR SCHOOLS/OUR SELVES

107 Earl Grey Rd.
Toronto, ON M4J 3L6
Canada
(416) 463-6978
Fax: (416) 463-6978
www.policyalternatives.ca/eduproj/o
sos.html

This magazine for Canadian education activists provides analysis of educational issues and information about activism.

OUR TIMES

1209 King St. W, Suite 201-A
Toronto, ON M6K 1G2
Canada
(800) 648-6131
Fax: (416) 531-7641
ourstory@web.net
www.ourtimes.web.net

Our Times: Canada's Independent Labour Magazine focuses on social change through unionism and democratic socialism.

OUT MAGAZINE

161 W University Pkwy. Box 12225
Jackson, TN 38308-10137
(212) 334-9119
Fax: (901) 668-7300
outmag@aol.com or sales@nbaf.com
nbaf.com

Out is a general interest gay and lesbian magazine.

PAKISTAN LINK

7545 Irvine Center Dr., Suite 100
Irvine, CA 92618-2934
(949) 789-7520
Fax: (949) 789-7515
editor@PakistanLink.com
www.pakistanlink.com

A paper focusing on issues related to Pakistan and Pakistani-Americans.

PAPERWORKER

P.O. Box 1475
Nashville, TN 37202
(615) 834-8590
Fax: (615) 831-6791
www.igc.apc.org/upiu

Paperworker is the official publication of the International Paperworkers' Union.

PARTNERS UPDATE
49 Powell St., Suite 500
San Francisco, CA 94102
(415) 981-1771
Fax: (415) 981-1991
panna@panna.org
www.igc.org/panna/about/pu.html

The publication of the Pesticide Action Network North America is circulated to its friends and supporters.

PATHFINDER
P.O.Box 649
Luck, WI 54853
(715) 472-4185
Fax: (715) 472-4184
nukewatch@lakeland.ws
www.nukewatch.com

Published by Nukewatch and the Progressive Foundation, *Pathfinder* encourages nonviolent change for an environment free of the nuclear industry and weapons of mass destruction.

PBI/USA REPORT
1904 Franklin St., Suite 505
Oakland, CA 94612
(510) 663-2362
Fax: (510) 663-2364
pbiusa@igc.org
www.wecaretoo.com/Organizations/CA/peace.html

This publication of the Peace Brigades International provides quarterly updates to the supporters of PBI in the U.S. about the work of peace teams in seven regions of the world. It is an information, outreach and fundraising tool.

PEACE MAGAZINE
P.O. Box 248, Station P
Toronto, ON M5S 2S7
Canada
(416) 533-7581
Fax: (416) 531-6214
mspencer@web.net
www.peacemagazine.org
Peace Magazine is a valuable resource for anyone wishing to keep abreast of the issues and activities of movements for peace and nonviolence around the world.

PEACE REVIEW: A TRANS-NATIONAL QUARTERLY
2130 Fulton St.
San Francisco, CA 94117
(415) 422-6349
Fax: (415) 422-2772
greens@usfca.edu
www.usfca.edu/politics/peacere-view.htm

Peace Review is a quarterly, multi-disciplinary, trans-national journal of research and analysis. Published by Peace and Justice Studies, University of San Francisco, it focuses on the current issues that underlie the promotion of a more peaceful earth.

PEACEWORK
2161 Massachusetts Ave.
Cambridge, MA 02140
(617) 661-6130
pwork@igc.org
www.afsc.org/peacewrk.htm

A monthly journal published since 1972, *Peacework* covers the full range of "Global Thought and Local Action for Nonviolent Social Change," with a special focus on the northeastern United States. It is meant to serve the movement as a trade journal, with minimal pretensions.

PERMACULTURE ACTIVIST, THE
P.O. Box 1209
Black Mountain, NC 28711
(828) 669-6336
Fax: (828) 669-5068
pcactiv@metalab.unc.edu
www.permacultureactivist.net/

The PA advocates and documents ecological design of housing, land-scapes and settlements as a tool supporting food and resource security, community empowerment, and local economic self-reliance.

PLANET DRUM PULSE, THE
P.O. Box 31251
San Francisco, CA 94131
(415) 285-6556
Fax: (415) 285-6563
planetdrum@igc.org
www.planetdrum.org

This biannual review, published by Planet Drum Foundation, focuses on issues of restoration ecology and the greening of cities.

PLOUGH READER
Spring Valley Bruderhof
Route 381 North
Farmington, PA 15437
(800) 521-8011
Fax: (724) 329-0914
feedback@plough.com
www.plough.com/usa/reader.htm

More than just a publishing venture,

Plough Reader serves a growing audience of open-minded readers who are dissatisfied with bland spirituality. Instead, it's a circle of peace and justice–oriented folk in which you, too, can have a part—as reader, critic and fellow seeker.

POCLAD: THE PROGRAM ON CORPORATIONS, LAW & DEMOCRACY

P.O. Box 246
S Yarmouth, MA 02664-0246
(508) 398-1145
Fax: (508) 398-1552
people@poclad.org
www.poclad.org

Published by the Council on International and Public Affairs, *POCLAD* is a quarterly publication that instigates democratic conversations and actions that contest the authority of corporations to govern.

POLISH-AMERICAN JOURNAL

1275 Harlem Rd.
Buffalo, NY 14206
(800) 422-1275
info@polamjournal.com
www.polamjournal.com

The *Polish American Journal* is the nation's largest English language, independent Polish-American monthly dedicated to the preservation and continuance of Polish-American culture in the U.S.

POOR MAGAZINE

255 9th Street
San Francisco, CA 94103
(415) 541-5629
tiny@poormagazine.org
www.poormagazine.org

POOR is the publication of a literary, visual arts-based community organization that provides vocational training, creative arts and literacy education to very low and no income adults and children in the San Francisco Bay area. Published by Poor News Network, it aims to deconstruct the margins of class and race oppression.

POZ MAGAZINE

349 West 12th Street
New York, NY 10014-1796
(800) 973-2376
Fax: (212) 675-8505
subscription@poz.com
www.poz.com

POZ focuses on quality of life issues for all those impacted by AIDS and HIV.

PR WATCH

520 University Ave., Suite 310
Madison, WI 53703
(608) 260-9713
Fax: (608) 260-9714
editor@prwatch.org
www.prwatch.org

Published by the Center for Media
and Democracy, *PR Watch* investi-
gates corporate and government
propaganda. The editors also wrote
*Toxic Sludge is Good For You and
Lies, Damn Lies and the Public
Relations Industry.*

PREVAILING WINDS MAGAZINE

P.O. Box 23511
Santa Barbara, CA 93121
(805) 899-3433
Fax: (805) 899-4773
patrick@silcom.com
www.prevailingwinds.org

Devoted to exposing assassination,
political scandals, medical fraud,
crime, media manipulation, corruption, mind control and high strange-
ness, *Prevailing Winds* is a publication of the Center for the
Preservation of Modern History.

PRINCETON PROGRESSIVE REVIEW

Princeton University
315 West College
Princeton, NJ 08544
progrev@phoenix.princeton.edu
www.princeton.edu/~progrev

A journal of news analysis and occa-
sional cultural critique voicing
social justice.

PRISON LEGAL NEWS

2400 NW 80th Street, PMB 148
Seattle, WA 98117
(206) 789-1022
Fax: (206) 505-9449
pln@prisonlegalnews.org
www.prisonlegalnews.org

PLN reports court rulings involving
prisoner rights and provides news
and commentary on criminal justice
issues.

PROBE

P.O. Box 1321, Cathedral Station
New York, NY 10025
(212) 647-0200
Fax: (212) 463-8002
probenewsletter.com

Probe is an investigative and inter-
pretive newsletter on science,
media, policy and health in the spirit of I. F. Stone. It promotes science
and rationality as key elements in a
democratic society.

PROGRESSIVE, THE
409 E Main St.
Madison, WI 53703
(608) 257-4626
Fax: (608) 257-3373
circ@progressive.org
www.progressive.org

The *Progressive* discusses peace,
politics, social justice and environmental concerns from a left of center point of view.

PROGRESSIVE LIBRARIAN
P.O. Box 2203, Times Square Station
New York, NY 10108
(973) 623-7642
web@libr.org
www.libr.org

A journal for critical studies and progressive politics, *Progressive
Librarian* brings to librarianship perspectives that challenge prevailing
assumptions concerning information
technology, library management,
censorship and other such issues.

PROGRESSIVE POPULIST, THE
P.O. Box 487
Storm Lake, IA 78715-0517
(512) 447-0455
populist@usa.net
www.populist.com

The *Progressive Populist* provides
monthly reports from the Heartland
on issues of interest to workers,

farmers and small business. It promotes the idea that people are more
important than corporations.

PROGRESSIVE REVIEW, THE
1312 18th Street NW, #502
Washington, DC 20036
(202) 835-0770
Fax: (202) 835-0779
news@prorev.com
emporium.turnpike.net/P/ProRev

This is Washington's most unofficial
source. It provides Green, populist
perspectives.

PROUD PARENTING
P.O. Box 8272
Van Nuys, CA 91409-8272
(818) 909-0314
Fax: (818) 909-3792
info@proudparenting.com
www.proudparenting.com

A magazine for today's gay, lesbian,
bisexual and transgendered parents
and their families.

PROUT JOURNAL, THE
7627 16th Street NW
P.O. Box 56466
Washington, DC 20040
(202) 829-2278
Fax: (202) 829-0462
proutwdc@igc.org
nysector@prout.org
prout.org

The *PJ* is a forum for linking spirituality and social issues, and elucidating upon the Progressive Utilization Theory (PROUT) For Personal and Planetary Transformation.

PSYCHOTHERAPY NETWORKER
Formerly the Family Therapy Networker
7705 13th Street NW
Washington, DC 20012
(202) 829-2452
Fax: (202) 726-7983
info@psychnetworker.org
www.psychotherapynetworker.org

PN presents alternative views of the psychotherapy environment.

PUBLIC CITIZEN MAGAZINE
1600 20th Street NW
Washington, DC 20009
(202) 588-1000
Fax: (202) 588-7799
pcmail@citizen.org
www.citizen.org

Public Citizen covers consumer rights, safety issues, corporate and business accountability, environmental issues and citizen empowerment.

PUBLIC EYE, THE
1310 Broadway, Suite #201
Somerville, MA 02144
(617) 666-5300
Fax: (617) 666-6622
pra@igc.org
www.publiceye.org/pra

The *Public Eye* is a quarterly newsletter of the Political Research Associates featuring an in-depth analysis and critique of issues pertaining to the U.S. political right wing.

QUILL
3909 N Meridian St.
Indianapolis, IN 46208
(317) 927-8000
Fax: (317) 920-4789
spj@spj.org
www.spj.org

A national publication of the Society of Professional Journalists, *Quill* reports on journalism.

RACE, POVERTY & THE ENVIRONMENT
Urban Habitat Program
San Francisco, CA 94129
(415) 561-3333
Fax: (415) 561-3334
contact@urbanhabitatprogram.org
www.urbanhabitatprogram.org/publications.htm

This national journal of the environmental justice movement is co-published with the Center for Race, Poverty and the Environment.

RACHEL'S ENVIRONMENTAL & HEALTH WEEKLY

P.O. Box 5036
Annapolis, MD 21403-7063
(410) 263-1584
Fax: (410) 263-8944 or (888) 272-2435
erf@rachel.org
www.rachel.org

Published by the Environmental Research Foundation, *Rachel's* provides timely information on toxic substances and other environmental hazards. It covers many technical issues, but is written in plain accessible language.

RADICAL AMERICA

P.O. Box 20735
Park West Station, NY 10025-1516
617/628-6585
Fax: 617/628-6585
http://pan.afrikan.net

Radical America is the publication of the Black Panther Collective.

RAISING BLACK & BIRACIAL CHILDREN MAGAZINE

13400 Madison Ave.
Lakewood, OH 44107
(310) 358-2932 or (800) 528-9648
info@magazinesofamerica.com
www.magazinesofamerica.com/rbbc

A quarterly publication geared toward black parents and parents of black and biracial children.

REASON FOUNDATION

3415 S Sepulveda Blvd., Suite 400
Los Angeles, CA 90034
(310) 391-2245
Fax: (310) 391-4395
gpassantino@reason.org
www.reason.org

Reason reports on public policy and culture from a libertarian perspective.

RELIGION WATCH

P.O. Box 652
North Bellmore, NY 11710
(516) 781-0835
Fax: Same
relwatch1@msn.com
www.religionwatch.com

This monthly newsletter monitors trends in contemporary religion.

RESPONSIVE PHILANTHROPY

National Committee for Responsive Philanthropy
2001 S Street NW, Suite 620
Washington, DC 20009
(202) 387-9177
Fax: (202) 332-5084
info@ncrp.org
www.ncrp.org

NCRP is committed to making philanthropy more responsive to socially, economically and politically disenfranchised people, and to the dynamic needs of increasingly diverse communities nationwide.

RETHINKING SCHOOLS

1001 E Keefe Ave.
Milwaukee, WI 53212
(800) 669-4192 or (414) 964-9646
Fax: (414) 964-7220
RS Business@aol.com
www.rethinkingschools.org

Rethinking Schools: An Urban Educational Journal provides an alternative to mainstream educational materials, and is committed to issues of equity and social justice.

REVOLUTIONARY WORKER

P.O. Box 3486, Merchandise Mart
Chicago, IL 60654
(773) 227-4066
Fax: (773) 227-4497
www.rwor.org

The weekly newspaper of the Revolutionary Communist Party, USA.

RIGHTS

666 Broadway, 7th Floor
New York, NY 10012
(212) 475-7206
Fax: (212) 614-6499
www.ccr-ny.org

Rights, published by the Center for Constitutional Rights, covers issues involving freedoms guaranteed by the Constitution and Bill of Rights.

ROLLING STONE

1290 Avenue of the Americas, 2nd Floor
New York, NY 10104
(212) 484-1616
Fax: (212) 767-8203
rollingstone.com
www.rollingstone.com

Rolling Stone is rock and politics at the cutting edge.

RUMINATOR REVIEW

1648 Grand Ave.
St. Paul, MN 55105
(651) 699-2610
review@ruminator.com
www.ruminator.com

This independent publication of MacAlester College is a nationally noted book review magazine.

RUSSIAN LIFE

P.O. Box 567
Montpelier, VT 05601-0567
(800) 639-4301
Fax: (802) 223-6105
sales@rispubs.com
www.russian-life.com

A 32-page color monthly magazine full of fascinating stories of Russian culture, history and life in the world's largest country, *Russian Life* celebrated its 40th birthday in October, 1996.

RYERSON REVIEW OF JOURNALISM
350 Victoria St.
Toronto, ON M5B 2K3
Canada
(416) 979-5319 x7434
1cunning@ryerson.ca
www.ryerson.ca/rrj

This progressive journalistic review is published by Ryerson Polytechnic University.

SAN FRANCISCO BAY VIEW
4908 3rd Street
San Francisco, CA 94124
(415) 671-0449
Fax: (415) 822-8971
editor@sfbayview.com
www.sfbayview.com

San Francisco Bay View is a national black newspaper.

SCANDINAVIAN PRESS/SWEDISH PRESS
P.O. Box 4302
Blaine, WA 98230
(604) 731-6381
Fax: (604) 731-2292
swepress@nordicway.com
www.nordicway.com

This quarterly publication is designed to provide up-to-date information from Denmark, Finland, Iceland, Norway and Sweden.

SECRECY & GOVERNMENT BULLETIN
1717 K Street NW, Suite 209
Washington, DC 20036
(202) 454-4691
Fax: (202) 675-1010
saftergood@fas.org
www.fas.org/sgp

A project of the Government Secrecy Federation of American Scientists, this publication reports on new developments in government secrecy policies.

SEJOURNAL
Published by Society of Environmental Journalists
P.O. Box 2492
Jenkintown, PA 19046
(215) 884-8174
Fax: (215) 884-8175
sej@sej.org
www.sej.org

The quarterly *SEJournal* is a publication written primarily by journalists for journalists. Its purpose is to provide information and guidance on covering the environment beat.

SENTIENT TIMES

P.O. Box 1330
Ashland, OR 97520
(541) 512-1084
Fax: (541) 512-1085
dmokma@jeffnet.org
www.sentienttimes.com

Sentient Times presents alternatives for personal and community transformation.

SHADOW, THE

P.O. Box 20298
New York, NY 10009
Shadow@MediaFilter.org
www.shadow.autono.net

New York City's only underground newspaper has been publishing steadily since March 1989. Most of our reporters, artists and photographers are from the Lower East Side, and all are committed political activists who share our mission to expose, inform and entertain readers with news, graphics and photos they will never see in the mainstream media.

SHELTERFORCE

National Housing Institute
439 Main St., Suite 311
Orange, NJ 07050-1523
(973) 678-9060
Fax: (973) 678-8437
yvonne@nhi.org
www.nhi.org

This national cross-disciplinary trade magazine for community builders offers mixed coverage of local stories, policy and theory to make useful links between community revitalization issues.

SIERRA MAGAZINE

P.O. Box 52968
Boulder, CO 80321-2968
(415) 977-5500
Fax: (415) 977-5799
information@sierraclub.org
www.sierraclub.org

A publication of the Sierra Club, America's most influential environmental grassroots advocacy organization founded in 1892, with a current membership of more than 700,000 members.

SKEPTIC

c/o Skeptics Society
P.O. Box 338
Altadena, CA 91001
(626) 794-3119
Fax: (626) 794-1301
skepticmag@aol.com
www.skeptic.com

Skeptic is the voice of science and critical thinking in the investigation of science, pre science, non science and nonsense.

SKEPTICAL INQUIRER

P.O. Box 703
Amherst, NY 14226-0703
(716) 636-1425
Fax: (716) 636-1733
info@csicop.org
www.csicop.org/si

Skeptical Inquirer is a magazine for science and reason.

SOCIAL ANARCHISM

Atlantic Center for Research and Education
2743 Maryland Ave.
Baltimore, MD 21218
spud@nothingness.org
www.nothingness.org/sociala

SA is a biannual anarchist journal with an intended bias towards the social over the individual—although in practice it tends towards eclecticism.

SOCIAL POLICY

25 West 43rd Street, Room 620
New York, NY 10036-7406
(212) 642-2929
Fax: (212) 642-1956
socpol@igc.apc.org
www.sclplcy@aol.com

Social Policy is a magazine about social movements. It breaks new ground with its in-depth and thoughtful analysis of public policy in America.

SOCIALIST REVIEW

1095 Market St, Suite 618
San Francisco, CA 94103
(415) 255-2296
socialistreview@earthlink.net
www.socialistreview.org

A forum for radical politics, cultural dissent and socialist critique.

SOJOURNER: THE WOMEN'S FORUM

42 Seaverns Ave.
Boston, MA 02130
(617) 524-0415
alisa@sojourner.org
www.sojourner.org

A forum for women to inform, challenge and encourage each other.

S.O.A. WATCH (WASHINGTON)

P.O. Box 4566
Washington, DC 20017
(202) 234-3440
Fax: (202) 636-4505
info@soaw.org
www.soaw.org

SOA Watch tracks and reports on activities at the School of the Americas.

SOJOURNERS
2401 15th Street NW
Washington, DC 20009
(202) 328-8842
Fax: (202) 328-8757
listserv@sojourners.com
www.sojo.net

Sojourners is a grassroots network for personal, community and political transformation rooted in prophetic biblical tradition.

SOLIDARITY
8000 E Jefferson
Detroit, MI 48214
(313) 926-5000
uaw@uaw.org
www.uaw.org

Solidarity is the official magazine of the United Auto Workers Union.

SOULS: A CRITICAL JOURNAL
Institute for Research in African-American Studies
Columbia University, 758
Schermerhorn Extension
Mail Code 5512
New York, NY 10027
(212) 854-7080
www.columbia.edu/cu/iraas/htm/iraas_souls.htm

In the spirit of W.E.B. DuBois, *Souls* is a quarterly interdisciplinary journal that is dedicated to the mapping of the intellectual contours of the modern black experience: the various ideological debates, politics, culture and recent history of African-American people.

SOUTH ASIA TIMES
38 Westland Ave., Suite 23
Boston, MA 02115
(617) 536-4606
Fax: (617) 536-4606
www.southasiatimes.com

This bimonthly newspaper provides necessary news and views on South Asia to general readers on the one hand, and valuable data and information on South Asian politics, economics, societies, arts and literature and other fields to researchers in various academic institutions on the other.

SOUTHERN EXPOSURE
P.O. Box 531
Durham, NC 27702-0531
(919) 419-8311 x26
Fax: (919) 419-8315
info@i4south.org
www.southernstudies.org

An award-winning magazine focused on fighting for a better South, *Southern Exposure* deals largely with corporations and labour issues in the American South.

SPIRIT OF CRAZY HORSE
P.O. Box 583
Lawrence, KS 66044
(785) 842-5774
Fax: (785) 842-5796
lpdc@idir.net
www.freepeltier.org/newspaper.htm

A bimonthly newspaper published by the Leonard Peltier Defense Committee, *Spirit of Crazy Horse* describes what to do to help free Leonard. Including statements from and updates on Leonard Peltier's case, it also focuses on native sovereignty and some prison issues.

ST. LOUIS JOURNALISM REVIEW
8380 Olive Blvd.
St. Louis, MO 63132
(314) 991-1699
Fax: (314) 997-1898
review@webster.edu
www.webster.edu/~review

SJR, the only local journalism review in the U.S., primarily critiques what is covered or ignored by the local media. It also covers some national and international news.

STAY FREE!
P.O. Box 306, Prince St. Station
New York, NY 10012
(718) 398-9324
Fax: (212) 477-5074

stayfree@sunsite.unc.edu
sunsite.unc.edu/stayfree

Stay Free! casts a critical eye on commercialism and pop culture.

STEELABOR
5 Gateway Center
Pittsburgh, PA 15222
(412) 562-2442
Fax: (412) 562-2445
webmaster@uswa.org
www.uswa.org/steelabor/JulAug00/j
ul_aug.htm

Steelabor offers news and commentary about members of steelworkers unions and covers political, economic and social issues of concern to steelworkers.

STUDENT PRESS LAW CENTER REPORT
1815 N Fort Meyer Dr., Suite 900
Arlington, VA 22209-1817
(703) 807-1904
Fax: (703) 807-2109
splc@splc.org
www.splc.org

This publication of the Student Press Law Center reports on cases, controversies and legislation relating to free press rights of student journalists. The center provides pro bono advice and legal assistance to involved students and educators.

SUN, THE
107 N Roberson St.
Chapel Hill, NC 27516
(919) 942-5282
info@thesunmagazine.org
www.thesunmagazine.org

This monthly alternative, literary magazine features essays, interviews, fiction, poetry and photographs.

SUSTAINABLE TIMES
1657 Barrington St., Suite 508
Halifax, NS B3J 2A1
Canada
(902) 423-6852
Fax: (902) 423-9736
ip-cuso@chebucto.ns.ca
reseau.chebucto.ns.ca/CommunityS
upport/CUSO/descrip.html

ST provides solutions to employment, environment and global development challenges.

SYNTHESIS/REGENERATION
P.O. Box 24115
St. Louis, MO 63130
(314) 727-8554
Fax: Call first
fitzdon@aol.com
www.greens.org/s-r

Synthesis/Regeneration: A Magazine of Green Social Thought is published tri-annually and focuses on the social aspects of environmentalism.

TASH NEWSLETTER
29 W Susuehanna Ave., Suite 210
Baltimore, MD 21204
(410) 828-8274
Fax: (410) 828-6706
aswann@tash.org
www.tash.org

Described by many as pioneers of social change for persons with disabilities underserved and undervalued in our society, the members of TASH are strong advocates of people whom have traditionally been denied access to education, work and community living.

TASK FORCE CONNECTIONS
973 Market St., Suite 600
San Francisco, CA 94103
(415) 356-8110
Fax: (415) 356-8138
info@cdcnpin.org
www.cdcnpin.org/connect/start.htm

Published by the National Task Force on AIDS Prevention, *Task Force Connections* provides updates and reports on issues related to AIDS prevention and treatment.

TEACHING TOLERANCE MAGAZINE

400 Washington Ave.
Montgomery, AL 36104
(334) 956-8200
Fax: (334) 264-3121
www.splcenter.org

Published by the The Southern Poverty Law Center, this biannual magazine covers issues related to the Teaching Tolerance Project begun by Morris Dees at the Southern Poverty Law Center.

TEAMSTER MAGAZINE

25 Louisiana Ave. NW
Washington, DC 20001
(202) 624-6800
Fax: (202) 624-6918
feedback@teamster.org
www.teamster.org

Published by the International Brotherhood of Teamsters, *Teamster Magazine* focuses on fighting for the future and the rights of working families in North America.

TEEN VOICES MAGAZINE

c/o Women Express P.O. Box 120-027
Boston, MA 02112-0027
(617) 426-5505
Fax: (617) 426-5577
womenexp@teenvoices.com
www.teenvoices.com

This journal of Women Express Inc. provides an interactive, educational forum that challenges media images of young women and girls.

TELEMEDIUM: THE JOURNAL OF MEDIA LITERACY

1922 University Ave.
Madison, WI 53705-4013
(608) 257-7712
Fax: (608) 257-7714
NTelemedia@aol.com
ddanenet.wicip.org/ntc/NTC.HTM

Telemedium promotes media literacy education with a positive, non-judgmental philosophy. Published by the National Telemedia Council, the oldest national media literacy organization in the U.S., it is in its 45th year.

TELEVISION PROJECT, THE

2311 Kimball St.
Silver Springs, MD 20910
(301) 588-4001
apluhar@tvp.org
www.tvp.org

This quarterly newsletter of Beyond TV aims to empower parents to use television wisely.

TEMP SLAVE

P.O. BOX 8284

Madison, WI 53708-8284

grvsmth@panix.com

www.panix.com/~grvsmth/redguide/slave.html

A mischievous and wildly amusing 'zine that documents the often unpleasant and bitter experiences of temp workers and the drudgery of the workplace.

TERRAIN

2530 San Pablo Ave.

Berkeley, CA 94702

(510) 548-2235

Fax: (510) 548-2240

terrain@ecologycenter.org

www.ecologycenter.org

A quarterly magazine focusing on environmental issues.

TEXAS OBSERVER, THE

307 West Seventh Street.

Austin, TX 78701

(800) 939-6620

Fax: (512) 477-0746

business@texasobserver.org

http://TexasObserver.org/

The *Observer* writes about issues ignored or underreported in the mainstream press, with the goal of covering stories crucial to the public interest and provoking dialogue that promotes democratic participation and open government.

THIRD WORLD RESURGENCE

Journal of the Third World Network

228 Macalister Rd.

Penang, Malaysia

+60(4)226-6728/6159

Fax: +60(4)226-4505

twn@igc.apc.org

www.twnside.org.sg

Third World Resurgence is the publication of an international network of groups and individuals involved in efforts to bring about a greater articulation of the needs and rights of people in the Third World; a fair distribution of world resources; and a utilization of ecologically sustainable forms of development that fulfill human needs.

THIS MAGAZINE

401 Richmond St. W, Suite. #396

Toronto, ON

Canada

(416) 979-9426

Fax: (416) 979-1143

thismag@web.net

www.thismag.org

Thirty-five years and still going strong, *This Magazine* is one of Canada's longest-publishing alternative journals. *This* focuses on Canadian politics, literature and culture and, in keeping with its radical roots, never pulls punches. Subversive, edgy and smart "Because Everything is Political," This is the real alternative to that.

TIBET PRESS WATCH
1825 K Street NW, Suite 520
Washington, DC 20006
(202) 785-1515
Fax: (202) 785-4343
ict@peacenet.org
www.savetibet.org

Tibet Press Watch, published by International Campaign for Tibet, focuses on the current situation inside Tibet as well as the support movement within the United States.

TIKKUN
2107 Van Ness Ave., Suite 302
San Francisco, CA 94109
(415) 575-1200
Fax: (415) 575-1434
Wehshamman@tikkun.com
www.tikkun.com
www.tikkun.ORG

Tikkun focuses on topics of particular interest to the Jewish community, including culture, politics, and philosophy.

TIMELINE
222 High St.
Palo Alto, CA 94301
(650) 328-7756
Fax: (650) 328-7785
timeline@globalcommunity.org
www. globalcommunity.org

Publisher of Timeline, the Foundation for Global Community is a project-based nonprofit educational organization that recognizes natural, social and economic systems as all parts of a single interconnected whole.

TIN HOUSE MAGAZINE
2601 NW Thurman St.
Portland, OR 97210
tinhouselq@aol.com
www.tinhouse.com

With its first issue in May 1999, *Tin House* was hailed by the *Village Voice* as "represent[ing] the future of literary magazines." A quarterly, Tin House has established itself as the new standard, where readers can expect the liveliest authors from a wide variety of genres and experiences, from Nobel laureates to new voices.

TO-DO LIST

P.O. Box 40128
San Francisco, CA 94140
todolist@todolistmagazine.com
www.todolistmagazine.com

Voted by the readers of Utne Reader as the Best New Magazine of 2000, *To-Do List* is "a magazine of meaningful minutiae" with an interest in diving into the details of daily life that make one click, roar, think, develop, and sometimes break down. Even in a decade where human DNA is becoming corporate property no one has the patent on these experiences. At *To-Do List* our outlook is broad, and our readers reflect that perspective.

TOWARD FREEDOM

The Independent Media
Convergence Project
P.O. Box 468
Burlington, VT 05402-0468
(802) 654-8024
Fax: (802) 658-3738
info@towardfreedom.com
www.towardfreedom.com

A progressive international news, analysis and advocacy journal that helps strengthen and extend human justice and liberties, *TF* opposes all forms of domination that repress human potential to reason, work creatively and dream.

TRANSITION

Harvard University
69 Dunster St.
Cambridge, MA 02138
(617) 496-2847
Fax: (617) 496-2877
transit@fas.harvard.edu
web-dubois.fas.harvard.edu/transition

An independent multicultural publication, declared by the *Nation* as "tremendously impressive... contain[ing] some of the smartest cultural criticism available anywhere."

TRANSITIONS RADIO MAGAZINE

2 Monte Alto Court
Santa Fe, NM 87505
(505) 466-2616
Fax: (505) 466-2617
host@transradio.com
www.transradio.com

Published by TransitionsMedia, *TRM* addresses social issues including the environment and ecology, new paradigms in responsible business, appropriate politics and government, healthcare and wellness, family, relationships and other topics not covered accurately or fairly by the mainstream media. TransitionsMedia also produces multimedia events, video interviews and video products for distribution on the above topics.

TREASURE STATE REVIEW
Published by: WOODFIRE Ashes
Press
106 2nd Street East, P.O. Box 4158
Whitefish, MT 59937
(406) 863-3221
Fax: 406-863-3333
blumberg@cyberport.net
www.nathanielblumberg.com

A Montana periodical devoted to
journalism and justice, *Treasure
State Review* is published by
WOODFIRE Ashes Press.
Established in 1991, it analyzes
press performance in the state and
the nation.

TREATMENT REVIEW
East Harlem HIV Care Network
HIV/ AIDS Information Outreach
Project
158 East 115th Street, Suite 218
New York, NY 10029
(212) 828-6141/42/43
Fax: (212) 360-5914
atdn@aidsnyc.org
www.aidsnyc.org/network

Treatment Review provides an
overview of AIDS treatments in
clinical trial, as well as general medical treatment information.

**TRICYCLE: THE BUDDHIST
REVIEW**
92 Vandam St.
New York, NY 10013
(212) 645-1143 and (800) 873-9871
www.tricycle.com

A magazine that explores Buddhism
and culture.

TRIPS: A TRAVEL JOURNAL
155 Filbert St., #245
Oakland, CA 94607
(510) 834-3433
office@tripsmag.com
www.tripsmag.com

Trips is a journal of real travelers.
It's for people who want to experience a place like the locals—staying
in the same areas, eating at the
same restaurants: for those who
don't care how many stars a hotel
has.

TRUE DEMOCRACY
P.O. Box 882
Lakebay, WA 98349-0882
(253) 884-0833
ajohnsonpresnsi@truedemocracy.net
truedemocracy.net/index.htm

Published by News Source Inc., *True
Democracy* aims to restore true
democracy to the United States and
the world. In addition, it features
research on the Trilateral
Commission.

TURNING THE TIDE: JOURNAL OF ANTI-RACIST ACTIVISM, RESEARCH AND EDUCATION

P.O. Box 1055
Culver City, CA 90232
(310) 288-5003
mnovicktttt@igc.ap.org
www.prisonactivist.org/pubs/ttt

This decade-old journal exposes the strategies of organized white supremacists and their roots in U.S. political, social and economic structures. It promotes anti-racist acitivism.

TYNDALL WEEKLY REPORT

135 Rivington St.
New York, NY 10002
(212) 674-8913
Fax: (212) 979-7304
andrew@tyndallreport.com
www.tyndallreport.com/tw0029.html

This weekly fax-sheet monitors the television networks' nightly newscasts.

UNABASHED LIBRARIAN, THE

P.O. Box 325
Mount Kisco, NY 10549
Fax: (914) 244-0941
editor@unabashedlibrarian.com
www.unabashedlibrarian.com

The "how I run my library good" newsletter for folks believing that "the library is more than information."

UPPNET NEWS

Labor Education Services, 437 Mgmt & Econ Bldg.
University of Minnesota
271 19th Avenue South
Minneapolis, MN 55455
(612) 624-4326
uppnet@labornet.org
www.mtn.org/jsee/uppnet.html

The official publication of the Union Producers and Programmers Network, *UPPNET News* promotes production and use of TV and radio shows pertinent to the cause of organized labor and working people.

URBAN ECOLOGIST QUARTERLY, THE

414 13th Street, Suite 500
Oakland, CA 94612
(510) 251-6330
Fax: (510) 251-2117
urbanecology@urbanecology.org
www.urbanecology.org

This magazine dedicated to creating ecologically and socially healthy communities highlights examples from throughout the world.

URBAN MO-ZA-IK

2729 Mission St., #201
San Francisco, CA 94110-3131
(415) 643-4401
Fax: (415) 643-4402

www.indypress.org/mstand/titles/urbanmozaik.html

The mission of *Urban Mo-Za-Ik* is to promote cross-cultural understanding and to celebrate the cultural diversity found in cities throughout North America.

URGENT ACTION NEWSLETTER
P.O. Box 1270
Nederland, CO 80466-1270
(303) 258-1170 or 1-303-258-7886
Fax: (303) 258-7881
sharris@igc.apc.org
www.amnestyusa.org/urgent

UAN is the newsletter of Amnesty International's Urgent Action Program Office.

U.S. BLACK ENGINEER AND INFORMATION TECHNOLOGY
729 E Pratt St., Suite 504
Baltimore, MD 21202
(410) 244-7101
Fax: (410) 752-1837
info@ccgmag.com
www.blackengineer.com

This quarterly dedicated to promoting opportunities for black Americans in science and technology provides interviews with successful minorities in business, education, science and technology. Those interviewed offer a balanced and realistic portrayal of engineering's

place in American society, and minority Americans' growing role in engineering.

UTNE READER
1624 Harmon Place, Suite 330
Minneapolis, MN 55403
(612) 338-5040
Fax: (612) 338-6043
info@utne.com
www.utne.com

A digest of alternative ideas and material reprinted from alternative and independent media sources.

VERDICT
Woolworth Building
233 Broadway, Suite 830
New York, NY 10279
(212) 346-7777

Verdict is a forum promoting involvement by legal professionals and others active in, or searching for, legal and organizational solutions to the problems facing our low-income communities. An official publication of the National Coalition of Concerned Legal Professionals, it explores the legal consequences flowing from complex systemic problems in our communities.

VETERAN, THE
8605 Cameron St., Suite 400
Silver Spring, MD 20910-3710
(301) 585-4000
Fax: (301) 585-0519
theveteran@vva.org
www.vva.org

The official voice of Vietnam
Veterans of America.

VIVA LA TORTUGA
P.O. Box 400
Forest Knolls, CA 94933
(415) 488-0370
Fax: (415) 488-0372
seaturtles@igc.org
www.seaturtles.org

Published by the Turtle Island
Restoration Network, *VLT* is the
newsletter of the Sea Turtle
Restoration Project.

VOICE OF REASON
P.O. Box 6656
Silver Spring, MD 20916
(301) 260-2988
Fax: (301) 260-2989
arlinc@erols.com
www.geocities.com/voiceofreason-
br/resources.htm

The newsletter of Americans for
Religious Liberty.

VOICES FROM THE EARTH
105 Standford SE,
P.O. Box 4524,
Albuquerque, NM 87106
(505) 262-1862
Fax: (505) 262-1864
admin@sric.org
www.sric.org

This quarterly journal of the
Southwest Research and
Information Center helps people
gain access to information vital for
asserting control over their lives.

WAR AND PEACE DIGEST
Journal of the War and Peace
Foundation
United Nations Bureau, 777 UN
Plaza
New York, NY 10017
(212) 557-2501
Fax: (212) 577-2515
warpeace@interport.net
www.warpeace.org

War and Peace Digest is an anti-
nuclear publication promoting
peace, social justice and media
reform.

WASHINGTON MONTHLY
Journal of Washington Monthly Co.
733 15th Street NW, Suite 1000
Washington, DC 20005
(202) 393-5155
Fax: (202) 332-8413

letters@washingtonmonthly.com
www.washingtonmonthly.com

A national opinion magazine covering politics, media and government.

WASHINGTON REPORT ON MIDDLE EAST AFFAIRS

P.O. Box 53062
Washington, DC 20009
(202) 939-6050
Fax: (202) 265-4574
info@washington-report.org
www.wrmea.com

The *Washington Report on Middle East Affairs* is a 140-page magazine published ten times annually in Washington, DC. It focuses on news and analysis from and about the Middle East and on U.S. policy in that region.

WASHINGTON SPECTATOR, THE

P.O. Box 20065
London Terrace Station
New York, NY 10011
(212) 741-2365
spectator@newslet.com
www.newslet.com/wash.specg

The *Washington Spectator* is a politically independent newsletter that reports on the vital issues of the day and tells "the real story" about what is going on in Washington.

WELFARE MOTHERS VOICE

2711 W Michigan
Milwaukee, WI 53208
(414) 342-6662
Fax: (414) 342-6667
wmvoice@execpc.com
www.execpc.com/~wmvoice

WMV is a voice for mothers and children in poverty who have joined together to be heard regarding all policies affecting families in poverty, the larger community and the Earth. *WMV* also covers activist movements related to poverty around the globe.

WHISPERING WIND

53196 Old Uneedus Rd.
P.O. Box 1390 Dept 3
Folsom, LA 70437-1390
(800) 301-8009
Fax: (985) 796-9236
www.whisperingwind.com

A bimonthly magazine dedicated to preserving the traditions of the American Indian, *Whispering Wind Magazine* since 1967 has brought its readers the crafts, material culture, history, powwow dates and reports of the American Indian in a scholarly, accessible format; expertly illustrated and photographed.

WHOLE EARTH MAGAZINE

P.O. Box 3000
Denville, NJ 07834-9879
(888) 732-6739
info@wholeearthmag.com
www.WholeEarthMag.com

Whole Earth Magazine provides access to tools, ideas, and practices; reviews books and products to help people help themselves; and publishes a catalogue.

WHY MAGAZINE

505 8th Avenue, Suite 2100
New York, NY 10018-0582
(212) 629-8850
Fax: (212) 465-9274
why@worldhungeryear.org
www.worldhungeryear.org/publications/why_mag.html

A quarterly publication that challenges the existance of hunger and poverty, *Why Magazine* presents leading thinkers and activists with information, insight, and opportunities for involvement.

W.I.G. MAGAZINE

6230A Wilshire Blvd., #72
Los Angeles, CA 90048
(206) 323-2369
mail@wigmag.com
www.wigmag.com/index.html

W.I.G.'s purpose is to encourage creative thinking among women by providing a forum for discussion, inspiration, shared wisdom, and adventure in the arts, music, sports and all aspects of women's culture. Wiggers tend to be the movers and shakers of women's youth culture, diving into everything they do.

WILD EARTH

The Journal of Wildlands Recovery and Protection
P.O. Box 455
Richmond, VT 05477
(802) 434-4077
Fax: (802) 434-5980
info@wild-earth.org
www.wild-earth.org

Wild Earth is dedicated to the restoration and protection of wilderness and biodiversity. We share a vision of an ecologically healthy North America—with adequate habitat for all native species, including vibrant, natural human communities.

WILD MATTERS

Formerly Food & Water Journal,
P.O. Box 543
Montpelier, VT 05601
(802) 229-6222
Fax: (802) 229-6751
info@foodandwater.org
www.wildmatters.org

Published by Food & Water Inc. ten times annually,*Wild Matters* advocates for safe food and water, and a clean environment by educating the public on the health and environmental dangers of food irradiation, genetic engineering and toxic pesticides.

WITNESS, THE

P.O. Box 1170
Rockport, ME 04856
(207) 763-2990
Fax: (207) 763-2991
office@thewitness.org
http://thewitness.org

The Witness is the only publication aimed at Episcopalians and the Anglican Communion that embraces—without equivocation—the liberation perspective that flows from the very core of Christian belief and values. We side with Jesus's radical claim that every person, every creature, every part of creation belongs to God and deserves the deepest respect and care.

WOMEN AND ENVIRONMENTS: INSTITUTE FOR WOMEN'S STUDIES AND GENDER STUDIES

New College, University of Toronto
IWSGS 40 Willcocks St.
Toronto, ON M5S 1C6
Canada
(416) 978-5259
Fax: (416) 946-5561
we.mag@utoronto.org
www.utoronto.ca/iwsgs/we.mag

WE International examines women's multiple relations to their environments, including built, social and natural feminist perspectives. Its editorial collective voluteer their time to edit and produce this contribution to feminist social change.

WOMEN'S EDUCATION DES FEMMES

256 Jarvis St. Suite 5A
Toronto, ON M5B 2J4
Canada
(416) 599-2854
Fax: (416) 599-5605
cclow@web.apc.org
www.nald.ca.org

Published by the Canadian Congress for Learning Opportunities for Women, this publication focuses on issues related to women in higher education.

WOMEN'S HEALTH LETTER
P.O. Box 467939
Atlanta, GA 31146-7939
(770) 668-0432
feedback@soundpub.com
www.ok.org/homemaker/pesach99/
healthpage.html

This thinking woman's guide to
wellness offers sane and sound
health and healing insights that are
often startlingly contrary to what
the medical industry would have us
believe.

**WOMEN'S REVIEW OF BOOKS,
WELLESLEY COLLEGE**
Published by the Center for
Research on Women
106 Central St.
Wellesley, MA 02481
(888) 283-8044
Fax: (781) 283-3645
lgardiner@wellesley.edu
www.wellesley.edu/womensrevie

A review of books by and about
women: fiction, nonfiction and poetry.

WORLD POLICY JOURNAL
New School University
66 5th Avenue, 9th Floor
New York, NY 10011
(212) 229-5808 x105
Fax: (212) 229-5579
levarts@newschool.edu
worldpolicy.org

A leading quarterly magazine covering international affairs in the
United States.

WORLD PRESS REVIEW
700 Broadway, 3rd Floor
New York, NY 10003
(212) 982-8880
worldpress@worldpress.org
www.worldpress.org

World Press Review is a digest of the
global press, presenting a sampling of
newspapers from around the world.

WORLD RIVERS REVIEW
Published by the International
Rivers Network
1847 Berkeley Way
Berkeley, CA 94703
(510) 848-1155
Fax: (510) 848-1008
irn@irn.org
www.irn.org

Reports the latest news on the
worldwide movement to stop
destructive dams. It provides information on alternatives to large
hydro projects and publishes action
alerts, book reviews and profiles of
key individuals and groups related
to this issue.

WORLD WATCH
P.O. Box 879
Oxon Hill, MD 20797
(888) 544-2303 and (310) 567-9522
Fax: (301) 567-9522
worlwatch@worldwatch.org
www.worldwatch.org

This bimonthly publication informs the general public about the damage done by the world economy to its environmental support system.

WORLDVIEWS
1515 Webster St., #305
Oakland, CA 94612
(510) 451-1742
Fax: (510) 835-3017
worldviews@igc.org
www.igc.org/worldviews

This quarterly journal of the WorldViews Resource Center reviews resources for education and action.

YES! A JOURNAL OF POSITIVE FUTURES
P.O. Box 10818
Bainbridge Island, WA 98110-0818
(206) 842-0216 and (800) 937-4451
Fax: (206) 842-5208
yes@futurenet.org
www.futurenet.org

A journal that helps shape and support the evolution of sustainable cultures and communities, *Yes!*

highlights ways that people are working for a just, sustainable and compassionate future.

YO! (YOUTH OUTLOOK)
660 Market St., Rm. 210
San Francisco, CA 94104
(415) 438-4755
Fax: (415) 438-4935
crew@youthoutlook.org
www.youthoutlook.org/

A weekly newsletter of writing and art by incarcerated youth.

YOGA JOURNAL
2054 University Ave., Suite 600
Berkeley, CA 94704
(510) 841-9200
Fax: (510) 644-3101
info@yogajournal.com
www.yogajournal.com

A bimonthly lifestyle magazine dealing with hatha yoga and wholistic healing.

YOUTH ACTION FORUM
Youth Action Network
761 Queen St. W, Suite 315
Toronto, ON M6J 1G1
Canada
(800) 718-LINK and (416) 368-2277
Fax: (416) 368-8354
695036@iran.net
www.youthactionnetwork.org

This youth activist publication is

dedicated to motivating and educating young people on the issues that are important to them.

Z MAGAZINE

18 Millfield St.
Woods Hole, MA 02543
(508) 548-9063
Fax: Call first
lydia.sargent@lbbs.org
sysop@zmag.org
www.lbbs.org

Z is an independent political magazine of critical thinking on political, cultural, social and economic life in the United States.

REGIONAL PUBLICATIONS

ACE MAGAZINE
486 W 2nd Street
Lexington, KY 40507
(859) 225-4889
Fax: (606) 226-0569
editor@acemagazine.com
www.aceweekly.com

ACLU NEWS
American Civil Liberties Union of
Northern California
1663 Mission St., 4th Floor
San Francisco, CA 94103
(415) 621-2493
Fax: (415) 621-3074
www.aclunc.org

AFRICAN VOICES
270 W 96th Street
New York, NY 10025
africanvoices@aol.com
africanvoices2.goemerchant2.com/
    nscgibin/africanvoices2/index.cgi?
    Merchant=africanvoices2

ARKANSAS TIMES
P.O. Box 34010
Little Rock, AR 72203
(501) 375-2985
Fax: (501) 375-3623
arktimes@arktimes.com
www.arktimes.com

ASIAN PAGES
P.O. Box 11932
St. Paul, MN 55111-0932
(952) 884-3265
Fax: (952) 888-9373
asianpages@att.net
www.asianpages.com

ASIAN REPORTER, THE
922 N Killingsworth St., Suite 1-A
Portland, OR 97217-2220
(503) 283-4440
Fax: (503) 283-4445
AR-news@juno.com
www.asianreporter.com

A weekly Asian newspaper reporting
international, national and local
Asian-related events.

ATHENS NEWS
14 N Court St.
Athens, OH 45701
(740) 594-8219
Fax: (740) 592-5695
anews@frognet.net
www.athennews.com

ATLANTA INQUIRER
947 M.L. King Drive,
N.W. Morris Brown Station
Atlanta, GA 30314
(404) 523-6086

news@theatlantainquirer.com
www.theatlantainquirer.com

AUSTIN CHRONICLE
P.O. Box 49066
Austin, TX 78765
(512) 454-5766
Fax: (512) 458-6910
Mail@auschron.com
www.auschron.com

BALTIMORE AFRO-AMERICAN
2519 North Charles St.
Baltimore, MD 21218
(410) 554-8200
Fax: (410) 554-8213
ammanuelm@afroam.org
www.afro.com

BALTIMORE CITY PAPER
812 Park Ave.
Baltimore, MD 21201
(410) 523-2300
Fax: (410) 523-2222
letters@citypaper.com
www.citypaper.com

BALTIMORE JEWISH TIMES
1040 Park Ave., Suite 200
Baltimore, MD 21117
(410) 752-3504
Fax: (410) 902-3317
webmaster@jewishtimes.com or
information@jewishtimes.com
www.jewishtimes.com

BAY NATURE
1328 6th Street, #2
Berkeley, CA 94710
(510) 528-8550
Fax: (510) 528-8117
baynature@baynature.com
www.baynature.com

BAY STATE BANNER
23 Drydock Ave.
Boston, MA 02210
(617) 261-4600
Fax: (617) 261-2346
www.baystatebanner.com

BAY WINDOWS
631 Tremont St.
Boston, MA 02118
(617) 266-6670
Fax: (617) 266-6973
letters@baywindows.com
www.baywindows.com

BECAUSE PEOPLE MATTER
A project of Sacramento
Community for Peace and Justice
403 21st Street.
Sacramento, CA 95814
(916) 444-3203
JeKeltner@aol.com

BIRMINGHAM WEEKLY
2101 Magnolia Ave. S, 4th Floor
Birmingham, AL 35205
(205) 322-2426
Fax: (205) 322-0040
sryan@bhamweekly.com

BLACK REIGN
40-A Wolkoff Lane
Staten Island, NY 10303
(718) 477-1630
Fax: (718) 477-1630
blackreignnews@yahoo.com
www.theblackreign.web.com

BOISE WEEKLY
109 South 4th Street
Boise, ID 83702
(208) 344-2055
Fax: (208) 342-4733
bingo@boiseweekly.com
www.boiseweekly.com

Boise Weekly is an alternative weekly covering local politics, social issues and entertainment, servicing Boise and the Treasure Valley.

BOSTON IRISH REPORTER
150 Mount Vernon St., Suite 120
Dorchester, MA 02125-3135
(617) 436-1222
www.bostonirish.com

BOSTON PHOENIX
126 Brookline Ave.
Boston, MA 02215
(617) 536-5390
Fax: (617) 859-8201
info@phx.com
www.bostonphoenix.com

New England's largest weekly newspaper, the *Boston Phoenix* has been a voice for alternative and progressive journalism since 1966.

BOULDER WEEKLY
690 South Lashley Lane
Boulder, CO 80303
(303) 494-5511
Fax: (303) 494-2585
wlaugesen@bolderweekly.com
www.boulderweekly.com

CALIFORNIA VOICE, THE
1791 Bancroft
San Francisco, CA 94124
(415) 671-1000
Fax: (415) 671-1005
www.sunreporter.com

An African-American weekly.

CALL AND POST (CLEVELAND)
118 Shaker Blvd.
Cleveland, OH 44120
(216) 791-7600
Fax: (216) 791-6568

An African-American weekly.

CALL AND POST (COLUMBUS)
109 Hamilton Ave.
Columbus, OH 43216
(614) 224-8123
Fax: (614) 224-8517

An African-American weekly.

CAMPAIGN FOR LABOR RIGHTS
1247 E Street SE
Washington, DC 20003
(541) 344-5410
Fax: (541) 431-0523
Clr2igc.org
www.summersault.con/~agj/clr

CANYON COUNTRY ZEPHYR, THE
P.O. Box 327
Moab, UT 84532
(435) 259-7773
Fax: (435) 259-7773
zephyr@lasal.net
www.canyoncountryzephyr.com

An alternative news source serving the canyonlands area of Utah and focusing on environmental issues in the area.

CAPE VERDEAN NEWS, THE (CVN)
P.O. Box 3063
New Bedford, MA 02741
(508) 997-2300
Fax: (508) 997-2300

This English-language newspaper, servicing the Cape Verdean-American community in southern New England, is published twice monthly.

CARIBBEAN TODAY
9020 SW 152nd Street
Miami, FL 33157
(305) 238-2868
Fax: (305) 252-7843
caribtoday@earthlink.net

CASCADIA TIMES
25-6 NW 23rd Place, #406
Portland, OR 97210
(503) 223-9036
Fax: (503) 736-0097
cascadia@spiritone.com
cascadia.times.org

Cascadia Times offers investigative journalism covering politics, environmental and other issues in the Pacific northwest.

CASCO BAY WEEKLY
11 Forest Ave.
Portland, ME 04101
(207) 775-6601
Fax: (207) 775-1615
editor@cbw.maine.com
www.cascobayweekly.com

CATALYST
332 South Michigan Ave., Suite 500
Chicago, IL 60604-4302
(312) 427-4830
Fax: (312) 427-6130
editorial@catalyst-chicago.org
www.catalyst-chicago.org

Catalyst is a monthly news magazine created in 1990 to document,
analyze and support improvement
efforts in Chicago's public schools.

CHAR-KOOSTA NEWS
P.O. Box 278, Hwy 93 North
Pablo, MT 59855
(406) 675-3000
Fax: (406) 675-2806

Chaar-Koosta News offers weekly
local coverage of the Confederated
Salish and Kootenai Tribes of the
Flathead Indian Reservation.

CHATHAN-SOUTHEAST CITIZEN
412 E 87th Street
Chicago, IL 60619
(773) 487-7700
Fax: (773) 487-7931
CCNG@interaccess.com

**CHEROKEE PHOENIX & INDIAN
ADVOCATE**
P.O. Box 948
Tahlequah, OK 74465
(918) 456-0671
Fax: (918) 458-6136

dagent@cherokee.org
www.cherokee.org

CHICAGO LIFE MAGAZINE
P.O. Box 11311
Chicago, IL 60611-0311
(773) 528-2737
chicagolifemag@mindspring.com

Covering politics, health and environmental issues with an emphasis
on improving quality of life.

CHICAGO READER
11 E Illinois St.
Chicago, IL 60611
(312) 828-0350
Fax: (312) 828-0305
mail@chireader.com
www.chicagoreader.com

CHICAGO WEEKEND
412 East 87th Street
Chicago, IL 60619
(312) 487-7700
Fax: (312) 487-7931

An African-American weekly.

CINCINNATI CITYBEAT
811 Race St., 5th Floor
Cincinnati, OH 45202
(513) 665-4700
Fax: (513) 665-4369
letters@citybeat.com
www.citybeat.com

CIRCLE, THE
P.O. Box 6026
Minneapolis, MN 55406
(612) 722-3686
Fax: (612) 722-3773
circlempls@aol.com
www.thecirclenews.org

A monthly publication of the
Minneapolis-St. Paul Native
American community.

**CITIZEN COMMUNITY
NEWSPAPERS**
412 East 87th Street
Chicago, IL 60619
(773) 487-7700
Fax: (773) 487-7931
ccng@interaccess.com
www.garthco.com-web

"The newspapers Chicago's black
community trusts."

CITY LIMITS
120 Wall St., 20th Floor
New York, NY 10005
(212) 479-3344
Fax: (212) 344-6457
nauer@citylimits.org
www.citylimits.org

New York's urban affairs and hous-
ing-policy paper.

CITY NEWSPAPER
250 N Goodman St
Rochester, NY 14607
(716) 244-3329
Fax: (716) 244-1126
ad_dept@rochester-citynews.com

CITY PAGES
401 North 3rd Street, Suite 550
Minneapolis, MN 55401
(612) 375-1015
Fax: (612) 372-3737
letters@citypages.com
www.citypages.com

CITY PAPER
812 Park Ave.
Baltimore, MD 21201
(410) 523-2300
Fax: (410) 523-8437
amarkowitz@citypaper.com
www.citypaper.com

CITYVIEW
100 4th Street
Des Moines, IA 50309
(515) 288-3336
Fax: (515) 288-0309
BPC@commonkink.com

CLEVELAND FREE TIMES
1846 Coventry Rd., Suite 100
Cleveland, OH 44118
(216) 321-2300
Fax: (216) 321-4456
www.freetimes.com

CLEVELAND JEWISH NEWS
3645 Warrensville Center Rd.
Cleveland, OH 44122-5294
(216) 991-8300
Fax: (216) 991-2088
www.clevelandjewishnews.com

COAST WEEKLY
668 Williams Ave.
Seaside, CA 93955
(831) 394-5656
Fax: (831) 394-2909
mail@coastweekly.com
www.bestofmontereycounty.com

COLORADO SPRINGS INDEPENDENT
121 E Pikes Peak, Suite 455
Colorado Springs, CO 80903
(719) 577-4545
Fax: (719) 577-4107
letters@csindy.com
www.csindy.com

COLUMBUS ALIVE
1079 N High St.
Columbus, OH 43201
(614) 221-2449
Fax: (614) 221-2456
alive@columbusalive.com
www.alivewired.com

COLUMBUS TIMES
2230 Buena Vista Rd.
Columbus, GA 31902
(706) 324-2404
Fax: (706) 596-0657

An African-American weekly.

COMMUNIQUE
Published by Florida Association of Voluntary Agencies for Caribbean Action
1310 N Paul Russeu Rd.
Tallahassee, FL 32301-5029
(850) 410-3100
Fax: (904) 942-5798
favaca@worldnet.att.net
www.favaca.org

The newsletter of Florida's unique development partnership with the Caribbean.

COMMUNITY CONTACT
5151 de Maisonneuve W, N.D.G.
Montreal, QC
CANADA
(514) 489-4540

An African-American monthly.

CONNECTIONS
Published by Peace and Justice
Network
P.O. Box 4123
Stockton, CA 95204
(209) 467-4455
dsteele@igc.apc.org
www.sonnet.com/usr/pjc

San Joaquin County's alternative
newspaper.

CONNECTIONS
P.O. Box 3866
Pagosa Springs, CO 81147
(970) 731-7070
Fax: (970) 731-7071
connections@pagosa.net

CONTEMPORA MAGAZINE
1501 Jefferson St.
Nashville, TN 37208
(615) 321-3268
Fax: (615) 321-0409
Tem37208@aol.com
Contemporamagazine.tipod.com

An African-American quarterly.

CREATIVE LOAFING
750 Willoughby Way
Atlanta, GA 30312
(404) 688-5623 and (704) 522-8334
Fax: (404) 614-3599 and (704) 522-8088
webmaster.creativeloafing.com
www.creativeloafing.com

**CYD JOURNAL: COMMUNITY
YOUTH DEVELOPMENT**
P.O. Box 33
Jamaica Plain, MA 02130
(617) 522-3435
Fax: (617) 522-3384
editor@newdesigns.org
www.cydjournal.org

*CYD Journal: Community Youth
Development* was previously known
as *New Designs For Youth
Development.*

DALLAS OBSERVER
P.O. Box 190289
Dallas, TX 75201
(214) 757-9000
Fax: (214) 757-8593
info@dallasobserver.com
www.dallasobserver.com

DAYTON VOICE
1927 N Main St.
Dayton, OH 45405
(937) 275-8855
Fax: (937) 275-6056
thevoice@commkey.net

DETROIT METRO TIMES
733 St. Antoine
Detroit, MI 48226
(313) 961-4060
Fax: (313) 961-6598
feedback@metrotimes.com
www.metrotimes.com

Metro Detroit's news, arts and culture weekly.

EAST BAY EXPRESS
1335 Stanford Ave.
Emeryville, CA 94608
(510) 879-3700
Fax: (510) 540-7700
Ebxpress.@aol.com
www.eastbayexpress.com

EASY READER
P.O. Box 427
Hermosa Beach, CA 90254
(310) 372-4611
Fax: (310) 318-6292
easyreader@earthlink.net

EAT THE STATE!
P.O. Box 85541
Seattle, WA 98145
(206) 903-9461
ets@scn.org
EatTheState.org

A forum for anti-authoritarian political opinion, research and humor.

ECONEWS
Published by the Northcoast Environmental Center
879 9th Street.
Arcata, CA 95521
(707) 822-6918
Fax: (707) 822-0827
nec@igc.org
www.necandeconews.to

One of the world's oldest bioregional newsletters, *ECONEWS* presents action-oriented and timely articles on forestry, wildlife, toxics, recycling, energy, endangered species, and air and water quality in northern California, the Pacific Northwest and beyond. It's all done in journalistic style, and leavened with humor and humanity.

EL BOHEMIO NEWS
4178 Mission St.
San Francisco, CA 94112
(415) 647-1924
Fax: (415) 824-7248

El Bohemio News, founded in 1971, is one of the oldest, most defined and reputable hispanic newspapers distributed throughout San Francisco and the Greater Bay area.

EL DIARIO/LA PRENSA
345 Hudson St., 13th Floor
New York, NY 10014
(212) 807-4600
Fax: (212) 807-4705

"*El Diario/La Prensa* continues to be the authentic voice and champion of Latino issues for the Tristate area's Latino community."

EL LATINO (SAN DIEGO)
Latina Enterprises
P.O. Box 550
San Diego, CA 92112
(619) 299-7744
Fax: (619) 299-7743

This regional, bilingual weekly, established in 1988, focuses on local Latino events.

EL OBSERVADOR
P.O. Box 1990
San Jose, CA 95109
(408) 453-2944
Fax: (408) 453-2979
sales@el-observador.com
www.el-observador.com

A bilingual weekly newspaper serving Hispanics in the San Francisco Bay area.

EL TECOLOTE
KQED
2601 Mariposa St.
San Francisco, CA 94110
(415) 864-2000
Fax: (415) 648-1046
commongroundradio.org

A bimonthly, bilingual tabloid designed to serve as a vehicle of information and organization to the Chicano/Latino communities of the Bay area, *El Tecolote* articulates their social, cultural, political and economic needs through ongoing and timely coverage of issues.

EUGENE WEEKLY
1251 Lincoln
Eugene, OR 97401
(541) 484-0519
Fax: (541) 484-4044
editor@eugeneweekly.com
www.eugeneweekly.com

EYE
471 Adelaide St. W
Toronto, ON
Canada
(416) 504-4339
Fax: (416) 504-4341
webmaster@eye.net
www.eye.net

Toronto's weekly newsmagazine.

FAIRFIELD/WESTCHESTER COUNTY WEEKLY
1 Dock St.
Stamford, CT 06902
(203) 406-2406
Fax: (203) 406-1066
fairfieldweekly.com or westchesterweekly.com
fairfieldweekly.com

FLAGPOLE MAGAZINE
112 S Foundry St.
Athens, GA 30601
(706) 549-9523
Fax: (706) 548-8981
mail@flagpole.com
www.flagpole.com

FLATLANDER, THE
P.O. Box 72793
Davis, CA 95617
(530) 750-FLAT
Fax: (530) 759-0404
www.flatland@dcn.davis.ca.us

FOLIO WEEKLY
9456 Phillips Highway, Suite 11
Jacksonville, FL 32256
(904) 260-9770
Fax: (904) 260-9773
themail@folioweekly.com
www.folioweekly.com

Northeast Florida's alternative news
and opinion magazine.

FORT WORTH WEEKLY
1204-B West 7th Street, Suite 201
Fort Worth, TX 76102
(817) 335-9559
Fax: (817) 335-9575
feedback@fwweekly.com
www.fwweekly.com

FREE TIMES
3105 Devine St.
Columbia, SC 29205
(803) 765-0707
Fax: (803) 765-0727
news@free-times.com
www.free-times.com

FULLERTON OBSERVER
P.O. Box 7051
Fullerton, CA 92834
(714) 525-6402
Observernewad@earthlink.net

Aims to inform Fullerton residents
about the institutions and other
societal forces that most impact
their lives, and to empower people
to participate in constructive ways.

**GAINESVILLE IGUANA/
ALACHUNE FREENET**
P.O. Box 14712
Gainesville, FL 32609
(352) 378-5655
help@afn.org
www.afn.org

A Gainesville weekly.

GAMBIT WEEKLY
3923 Bienville St.
New Orleans, LA 70119
(504) 486-5900
Fax: (504) 483-3159
response@gambitweekly.com
www.bestofneworleans.com

GLUE L.A.
171 Pier Ave., Suite 236
Santa Monica, CA 90405
(310) 392-1391
Fax: (310) 392-6374
gluela@aol.com
www.cridder.com/glue

An independent weekly dedicated to unifying social activism across the many cultural, economic and ethnic populations in Los Angeles.

GLYPH
117 E Louisa, #253
Seattle, WA 98102
(206) 343-5650
Fax: (206) 343-7135
Chaosunit@aol.com

Monthly tales of highbrow pulp.

GREAT GOD PAN
P.O. Box 491
Hermosa Beach, CA. 90254-0491
pan@cyberverse.com

A 122-page journal about California that is definitely not one of those glossy travel magazines that look like they're written by the Chamber of Commerce.

GREEN CITY CALENDAR, THE
Published by Planet Drum
P.O. Box 31251
San Francisco, CA 94131
(415) 285-6556

Fax: (415) 285-6563
planetdrum@igc.org

A comprehensive listing of Bay area ecological events, with a changing thematic focus each issue.

GREEN CITY PROJECT
1910 Mission St.
San Francisco, CA 94103
(415) 701-9864
Fax: (415) 701-9865
greencity@igc.org
www.green-city.org

Dedicated to increasing the compatibility of cities with the natural environment by providing resources such as our online calendar, volunteer network, and education-action program.

HARTFORD ADVOCATE
100 Constitution Plaza
Hartford, CT 06103
(860) 548-9300
Fax: (860) 548-9335
hartfordadvocate.com
www.hartfordadvocate.com

HEADWATERS
P.O. Box 729
Ashland, OR 97520
(541) 482-4459
Fax: (541) 482-7282
info@headwaters.org
www.headwaters.org

A bimonthly newsletter.

HIGHBRIDGE HORIZONS
979 Ogden Ave.
Bronx, NY 10452
(718) 293-4352
information@highbridge.org
www.highbridgelife.org

A newsletter to assist residents of the Highbridge neighborhood in the Bronx in taking charge of their lives and improving the lives of their friends and neighbors.

HISPANIC: BUSINESS, CAREER, POLITICS & CULTURE
1406 Camp Crapft Rd., Suite 103
Austin, TX 78746
(512) 476-5599

HOMELESS GAZETTE NEWSLETTER, THE; HOMELESS REPORTER NEWS-SHEET, THE
P.O. Box 1053
Dallas, TX 75221
writzstuff1953@yahoo.com

Editorializes homelessness and poverty issues. Editor and publisher Bill Mason also edits *The Homeless Reporter News-sheet*.

HONOLULU WEEKLY
1200 College Walk
Honolulu, HI 96817
(808) 528-1475
Fax: (808) 528-3144
honoluluweekly.com

HOUR MAGAZINE
4130 Saint-Denis
Montreal, QC
Canada
(514) 848-0777
Fax: (514) 848-9004
www.hour.com

HOUSTON PRESS
1621 Milam, Suite 100
Houston, TX 77002
(713) 280-2400
Fax: (713) 280-2444
feedback@houstonpress.com
www.houstonpress.com

ILLINOIS TIMES
P.O. Box 3524
Springfield, IL 62708
(217) 753-2226
Fax: (217) 753-2281
editor@illinoistimes.com
illtimes@midwest.net

IMPACT WEEKLY
1927 N Main St.
Dayton, OH 45405
(937) 275-8855
Fax: (937) 279-1754
impactweekly@commkey.net

Alternative newsweekly covering the Greater Dayton region.

IMPACTO: THE LATIN NEWS
853 Broadway, Suite 811
New York, NY 10003
(212) 505-0288
Fax: (212) 598-9414

IN PITTSBURGH NEWSWEEKLY
2000 E Carson St.
Pittsburgh, PA 15203
(412) 488-1212
Fax: (412) 488-1217
info@inpgh.com
www.inpgh.com

INDEPENDENT WEEKLY
P.O. Box 2690
Durham, NC 27715
(919) 286-1972
Fax: (919) 286-4274
actnow@indyweek.com
www.indyweek.com

INDIA ABROAD
43 West 24th Street, 17th Floor
New York, NY 10010
(212) 929-1727
Fax: (212) 627-9503

India Abroad is one of the leading
newspapers for Indians living in
America, Canada and England.

INDIA IN NEW YORK
43 West 24th Street
New York, NY 10010
(212) 929-1727

Fax: 212) 627-9503
mail@indiaabroad.com
www.indiainnewyork.com

INDIANAPOLIS RECORDER
2901 N Tacoma Ave.
Indianapolis, IN 46218
(317) 924-5143
Fax: (317) 924-5148
newsroom@indyrecorder.com
www.indianapolisrecorder.com

Since 1895 *Indianapolis Recorder*
has been the state's greatest weekly
newspaper, preparing a conscious
community today and beyond.

INSIDE MAGAZINE
2100 Arch St. 4th Floor
Philadelphia, PA 19103
(215) 832-0700
Fax: (215) 569-3389
www.jewishexponent.com

Quarterly publication of the Jewish
Federation of Greater Philadelphia.

INSIDE THE ISLANDER
1003 E Trent, Suite 110
Spokane, WA 99202
(509) 325-0634
Fax: (509) 325-0638
letters@inlander.com
www.inlander.com

INTERMOUNTAIN JEWISH NEWS

1275 Sherman St.
Denver, CO 80203-2299
(303) 861-2234
Fax: (303) 832-6942
hillel@ijn.com
www.ijn.com

Jewish news for middle America.

IRISH HERALD

2145 19th Avenue, #203
San Francisco, CA 94116-1866
(415) 665-6653
Fax: (415) 665-9566
editor@irish-herald.com.
irishherald.com

ISTHMUS

101 King St.
Madison, WI 53703
(608) 251-5627
Fax: (608) 251-2165
edit@isthmus.com
www.thedailypage.com

ITHACA TIMES

P.O. Box 27
Ithaca, NY 14851
(607) 277-7000
Fax: (607) 277-1012
ithtimes@aol.com

JACKSONVILLE FREE PRESS, THE

903 Edgewood Ave W
Jacksonville, FL 32208
(904) 634-1993
jfreepress@aol.com

A weekly African-American newspaper.

JAM RAG

P.O. Box 20076
Ferndale, MI 48220
(248) 542-8090
Fax: (248) 542-9826
jamrag@genie.com

A local activist publication in the Detroit area, *Jam Rag* has been very active with community radio issues, Green issues and the Alliance Democracy.

JEWISH ADVOCATE, THE

15 School St.
Boston, MA 02108
(617) 367-9100
Fax: (617) 367-9310

JEWISH BULLETIN
225 Bush St., Suite 1480
San Francisco, CA 94104-4281
(415) 263-7200
Fax: (415) 263-7223
letters@jbnc.com
www.jewishsf.com

An English-language weekly newspaper covering the Jewish community, Jewish events (local, state, national, global) and Jewish people.

JEWISH EXPONENT
226 South 16th Street
Philadelphia, PA 19102
(215) 893-5700
Fax: (215) 790-0087

JEWISH JOURNAL
601 Fairway Dr.
Deerfield Beach, FL 33441
(954) 752-7474
Fax: (954) 752-7855

JEWISH NEWS OF GREATER PHOENIX
1625 E Northern Ave., Suite 106
Phoenix, AZ 85020-3979
(602) 870-9470
Fax: (602) 870-0426
editor@jewishaz.com
www.jewishaz.com

JEWISH PRESS, THE
333 South 132nd Street
Omaha, NE 68154-2198
(402) 334-8200
Fax: (402) 334-5422
www.jewishomaha.org

JOURNAL VOIR
355 Ste-Catherine Ouest, 7th Floor
Montreal, QC H3B 1A5
Canada
(514) 848-0805
Fax: (514) 848-9004
www.voir.ca

Free weekly published every Thursday with 120,000 copies distributed in the Greater Montreal area.

JUST OUT
P.O. Box 14400
Portland, OR 97293-0400
(503) 236-1252
Fax: (503) 236-1257
justout@justout.com
www.justout.com

LA GACETA
P.O. Box 5536
Tampa, FL 33675
(813) 248-3921
Fax: (813) 247-5357
Lagaceta@aol.com

A local paper published in Spanish, English and Italian.

LA OPINION

411 West 5th Street
Los Angeles, CA 90013-1000
(213) 622-8332
Fax: (213) 622-2177

A local Spanish daily since 1926.

LA PRENSA

685 South Compton Rd, 27th Floor
Longwood, FL 32750
(407) 767-0070
Fax: (407) 767-5478

Local Spanish-language weekly.

LA PRENSA DE SAN ANTONIO

318 S Flores St.
San Antonio, TX 78204
(210) 242-7900
Fax: (210) 242-7901
tduran@laprensa.com
www.laprensa.com

Local bilingual weekly.

LA VOZ DE COLORADO

2885 West 3rd Avenue
P.O. Box 19310
Denver, CO 80219
(303) 936-8556
Fax: (303) 922-9632
lavoz@rmi.net

A regional bilingual weekly newspaper published to serve the communication needs of the Hispanic community in the Denver, Colorado area.

LA VOZ DE HOUSTON

6101 Southwest Fwy., Suite 127
Houston, TX 77057
(713) 664-4404
Fax: (713) 664-4414
adf@lavozdehouston.com

L.A. WEEKLY

P.O. Box 4315
Los Angeles, CA 90078
(323) 465-4433
Fax: (213) 465-0044
letters@laweekly.com
www.laweekly.com

L.A. YOUTH

5967 West 3rd Street, Suite 301
Los Angeles, CA 90036
editor@layouth.com
www.layouth.com

The newspaper by and about Los Angeles teens.

LABOR/COMMUNITY ALLIANCE

P.O. Box 5077
Fresno, CA 93755
(559) 226-0477
Fax: (559) 226-3962
allianceeditor@attbi.com
www.fresnoalliance.com/home

An independent voice for workers and progressive groups in Fresno and the Central San Joaquin Valley, supporting the struggle for social and economic justice and a living wage.

LEO: LOUISVILLE ECCENTRIC OBSERVER
600 E Main St., Suite 102
Louisville, KY 40202
(502) 895-9770
Fax: (502) 895-9779
michael@louisville.com
www.louisville.com/leo.html

LOS ANGELES SENTINEL
3800 Crenshaw Blvd.
Los Angeles, CA 90008
(323) 299-3800
Fax: (323) 299-3896

An African-American weekly.

MEDIAFILE
Published by Media Alliance
814 Mission St., Suite 205
San Francisco, CA 94103
(415) 546-6334
Fax: (415) 546-6218
ma@igc.org
www.media-alliance.org

Mediafile presents independent reviews of Bay area media, including publications, broadcast outlets and Internet publishing.

MEMPHIS FLYER
460 Tennessee St.
Memphis, TN 38103
(901) 521-9000
Fax: (901) 521-0129
letters@memphisflyer.com
www.memphisflyer.com

METRO
550 South 1st Street
San Jose, CA 95113
(408) 298-8000
Fax: (408) 298-6992
webmaster@metroactive.com
metroactive.com

A Bay area arts and entertainment service of Metro Newspapers.

METRO PULSE
505 Market St., Suite 300
Knoxville, TN 37902
(865) 522-5399
Fax: (423) 522-2955
info@metropulse.com
www.metropulse.com

METRO SANTA CRUZ
115 Cooper St.
Santa Cruz, CA 95060
(831) 457-9000
Fax: (831) 457-5828
msc@metcruz.com
www.metcruz.com

METROLAND
4 Central Ave., 4th Floor
Albany, NY 12210
(518) 463-2500
Fax: (518) 463-3712
result@metroland.com
www.metroland.com

An alternative newsweekly serving Albany and the surrounding area.

MIAMI NEW TIMES
2800 Biscayne Blvd., Suite 100
Miami, FL 33137
(305) 576-8000
Fax: (305) 571-7676
editorial@miami-newtimes.com
www.miaminewtimes.com

MIAMI TIMES
900 NW 54th Street
Miami, FL 33127
(305) 757-1147
Fax: (305) 756-0771
miamit@aol.com

For more than seven decades, the *Miami Times* has reported faithfully each week on the African-American community of Dade County.

MICHIGAN CHRONICLE
479 Ledyard St.
Detroit, MI 48201-2867
(800) 203-2229
Fax: (313) 963-8788
chronicle4@aol.com

An African-American weekly since 1936.

MICHIGAN CITIZEN
211 Glendale, Suite 216
P.O. Box 03560
Highland Park, MI 48203
(313) 869-0033
Fax: (313) 869-0430
webmaster@michigancitizen.com
www.michigancitizen.com

The largest black-owned newspaper in Michigan and America's most progressive newspaper.

MISSOULA INDEPENDENT
115 South 4th West
P.O. Box 8275
Missoula, MT 59801
(406) 543-6609
Fax: (406) 543-4367
info@everyweek.com
www.everyweek.com

Western Montana's weekly journal.

MONDAY MAGAZINE
818 Broughton St.
Victoria, BC V8W 1E4
Canada
(250) 382-6188
Fax: (250) 381-2662
sales@monday.com
www.monday.com

MONTREAL MIRROR
400 McGill St., #100
Montreal, QC H2V 2G1
Canada
(514) 393-1010
Fax: (514) 393-3173
mirror@babylon.montreal.qc.ca
www.montrealmirror.com

MOUNTAIN XPRESS
P.O. Box 144
Asheville, NC 28802
(828) 251-1333
Fax: (828) 251-1311
publisher@mountainx.com
www.mountainx.com

A free alternative weekly.

MUNDO HISPANICO
P.O. Box 13808
Atlanta, GA 30324-0808
(404) 881-0441
Fax: (404) 881-6085

A local bilingual weekly.

NATIVE NEWS
719 East 11th Avenue, Suite C
Anchorage, AK 99501
(907) 258-8880
Fax: (907) 258-8805
nnn@nativenews.net
www.nativenews.net

"*Native News* reports Native American-specific news, publishes action alerts pertinent to our various nations and provides a news feed for newpapers and radio stations."

NAVAJO TIMES
P.O. Box 310
Window Rock, AZ 86515-0310
(928) 871-6641
Fax: (928) 871-6409
nt@primenet.com
www.thenavajotimes.com

A local American Indian weekly.

NEW HAVEN ADVOCATE
1 Long Wharf Dr.
New Haven, CT 06511
(203) 789-0010
Fax: (203) 787-1418
newhadvo@pcnet.com
newhavenadvocate.com

NEW PITTSBURGH COURIER
315 E Carson St.
Pittsburgh, PA 15219
(412) 481-8302
Fax: (412) 481-1360

A twice-weekly African-American
newspaper.

**NEW TIMES, BROWARD-PALM
BEACH**
16 NE 4th Street, Suite 200
Ft. Lauderdale, FL 33301
(954) 233-1600
Fax: (954) 233-1571
feedback@newtimesbpb.com
www.newtimesbpb.com

News, entertainment and investigative journalism.

NEW TIMES, LOS ANGELES
1950 Sawtelle Blvd., Suite 200
Los Angeles, CA 90025
(310) 477-0403
editor@newtimesla.com
newtimesla.com

NEW YORK BEACON, THE
15 East 33rd Street
New York, NY 10016
(212) 213-8585
Fax: (212) 213-6291

A weekly tabloid catering to New
York's minority populations of
African Americans, Hispanics and
Caribbeans

NEW YORK PRESS
333 7th Avenue, 14th Floor
New York, NY 10001
(212) 244-2282
Fax: (212) 244-9864
submissions@nypress.com
www.nypress.com

NEWCITY
770 N Halsted, Suite 306
Chicago, IL 60622
(312) 243-8786
Fax: (312) 243-8802
letters@newcitynet.com
elaine@newcitynet.com
www.newcitynet.com

Chicago's alternative weekly.

**NEWS FROM NATIVE
CALIFORNIA**
P.O. Box 9145
Berkeley, CA 94610
(510) 549-2802
Fax: (510) 549-1889
news@heydaybooks.com
www.heydaybooks.com/news

California's only quarterly magazine
devoted entirely to the state's
Native people.

NEWTIMES, SAN LUIS OBISPO
505 Higuera St.
San Luis Obispo, CA 93401
(805) 546-8208
Fax: (805) 546-8641
mail@newtimesslo.com
www.newtimesslo.com

NIKKEI WEST
P.O. Box 2118
Cupertino, CA 95015
(408) 998-0920 x4916
mail@nikkeiwest.com
www.nikkeiwest.com

Japanese American community
newspaper published twice monthly.

NORTH AMERICAN POST
662 1/2 S Jackson St.
Seattle, WA 98104
(206) 624-4169
Fax: (206) 625-1424
hokubei@msn.com
www.napost.com
An Asian weekly.

NORTH BAY PROGRESSIVE
P.O. Box 14384
Santa Rosa, CA 95402
(707) 525-1422
Fax: (707) 595-4700
www.northbayprogressive.org

Regional biweekly covering local,
national and international news:
"All the News That Didn't Fit."

NORTH COAST XPRESS
P.O. Box 1226
Occidental, CA 95465
(707) 874-3104
Fax: (707) 874-1453
doretk@sonic.net
www.north-coast-
xpress.com/~doretk

NCX supports grassroots movements and under-represented
minorities. It exposes threats to the
environment, the unjust criminal
justice system and corporate control
of politics and the economy.

NORTH KITSAP HERALD
A division of Sound Publishing Inc.
18887 Hwy 305, Suite 700
Poulsbo, WA 98370
(360) 779-4464
Fax: (360) 779-8276
jshaw@northkitsapherald.com

**NORTHERN CALIFORNIA
BOHEMIAN**
50 Mark West Springs Rd.
Santa Rosa, CA 95403
(707) 527-1200
Fax: (707) 521-1966
editor@bohemian.com
www.metroactive.com/sonoma

Northern California Bohemian is a
forum for art and issues, both
regional and national in scope.

NORTHWEST ASIAN WEEKLY

P.O. Box 3648
Seattle, WA 98114
(206) 223-5559
Fax: (206) 223-0626
scpnwana@nwlink.com
www.nwasianweekly.com

NOW MAGAZINE

189 Church St.
Toronto, ON M5B 1V7
Canada
(416) 364-1300
Fax: (416) 364-1433
letters@nowtoronto.com or
news@toronto.com
www.nowtoronto.com

Toronto's independent weekly news-magazine.

NUVO NEWSWEEKLY

811 E Westfield Blvd.
Indianapolis, IN 46220
(317) 254-2400
Fax: (317) 254-2405
nuvo@nuvo.net
www.nuvo-online.com

Newsweekly offering the city's most authoritative coverage of politics, culture, the arts and music—provocative and literate.

OAKLAND POST

630 20th Street
Oakland, CA 94612
(510) 287-8200
Fax: (510) 763-9670
www.oakpostonline.com

OC WEEKLY

P.O. Box 10788
Costa Mesa, CA 92626
(714) 708-8408
Fax: (714) 708-8410
letters@ocweekly.com
www.ocweekly.com

OJIBWE NEWS, THE

1106 Paul Bunyan Drive NE
Bemidji, MN 56601
(218) 751-1655
Fax: (218) 251-0650

Weekly Native news with a focus on reservation and urban American Indian communities within Minnesota.

OKLAHOMA GAZETTE

3701 N Shartel Ave.
Oklahoma City, OK 73118
(405) 528-6000
Fax: (405) 528-4600
www.okgazette.com

OMAHA READER
4807 Dodge St.
Omaha, NE 68132
(402) 341-7323
Fax: (402) 341-6967
reader@synergy.net
www.thereader.com

OREGON PEACE WORKER, THE
104 Commercial St. NE
Salem, OR 97301
(503) 371-8002
Fax: (503) 588-0088
pbergel@peacenet.org
www.oregonpeaceworks.org

Ten times a year the *Oregon Peace Worker* publishes peace, justice and environmental articles that are regional, national and international in scope.

ORLANDO WEEKLY
111 W Jefferson St., Suite 200
Orlando, FL 32801-1823
(407) 377-0400
Fax: (407) 377-0420
feedback@orlandoweekly.com
www.orlandoweekly.com

A division of the Times-Shamrock Group, *Orlando Weekly* is an alternative news publication, also published as the Web 'zine orlandoweekly.com. Times-Shamrock newsrooms reflect the diversity found in the communities they serve, promoting progressive social change.

OTHER PAPER, THE (TOP)
P.O. Box 11376
Eugene, OR 97440
(541) 345-6350
top_staff@efn.org
www.efn.org/~topaper

OTTAWA XPRESS
69 Sparks St.
Ottawa, ON K1P 5M5
Canada
(613) 237-8226
Fax: (613) 232-9055
www.theottawaxpress.ca

PACIFIC NORTHWEST INLANDER
1020 W Riverside
Spokane, WA 99201
(509) 325-0634
Fax: (509) 325-0638
inlander@iea.com
www.inlander.com

PACIFIC SUN
21 Corte Madera Ave.
Mill Valley, CA 94941
(415) 383-4500
Fax: (415) 383-4159
PSUN@aol.com
www.pacificsun.com

PAPER, THE
959 Lake Dr.
Grand Rapids, MI 49506
(616) 559-0210
Fax: (616) 559-0213
adinfo@the-paper.com
www.the-paper.com

PDXS: PULSE OF PORTLAND
P.O. Box 10046
Portland, OR 97296
(503) 224-7316
pdxs@teleport.com
www.pdxs.com

PHILADELPHIA CITY PAPER
123 Chestnut St., 3rd Floor
Philadelphia, PA 19106
(215) 735-8444
Fax: (215) 735-8535
adinfo@citypaper.net
www.citypaper.net

PHILADELPHIA TRIBUNE, THE
520 South 16th Street
Philadelphia, PA 19146
(215) 893-4050
Fax: (215) 735-3612
www.phila-tribune.com
An African-American weekly.

PHOENIX NEW TIMES
1201 E Jefferson St.
Phoenix, AZ 85034
(602) 271-0040
Fax: (602) 495-9954
newtimes@newtimes.com
www.phoenixnewtimes.com

PITCH WEEKLY
1701 Main St.
Kansas City, MO 64108
(816) 561-6061
Fax: (816) 756-0502
pitch@pitch.com
www.pitch.com

The weekly alternative newspaper
of metro Kansas City.

POINT
P.O. Box 8325
Columbia, SC 29202
(800) 849-1803
Fax: (803) 808-3781
scpoint@mindspring.com
www.scpronet.com/point/index.html

South Carolina's independent news-
monthly.

PORTLAND ALLIANCE, THE
Published by Northwest Alliance for
Alternative Media and Education
2807 SE Stark St.
Portland, OR 97214
(503) 239-4991
Fax: (503) 232-3764
alliance@teleport.com
www.teleport.com/~alliance

Progressive community news.

PORTLAND FREE PRESS
P.O. Box 1327
Tualatin, OR 97062
(503) 675-3051

PRECINCT REPORTER
1677 W Baseline St.
San Bernadino, CA 92411
(909) 889-0597
Fax: (909) 889-1706

A publication serving the African-American,Caribbean and African communities.

PROPER GANDER... Articomics and Such
P.O. Box 434
San Marcos, TX 78667
(512) 392-4728
propergander@sanmarcos.net

A regional alternative art and social commentary newspaper.

PROVIDENCE PHOENIX
150 Chestnut St.
Providence, RI 02903
(401) 273-6397
Fax: (401) 351-1399
www.providencephoenix.com

PULSE OF THE TWIN CITIES
3200 Chicago Ave.
Minneapolis, MN 55407
(612) 824-0000
Fax: (612) 822-0342

editor@pulsetc.com
www.pulsetc.com

PUTNAM PIT, THE
P.O. Box 1483
Cookeville, TN 38503
(530) 504-6613
geoff@putnampit.com
www.putnampit.com

The watchdog of the Upper Cumberland, Putnam County.

QUAKE
809 West 9th Street
Russellville, KY 42276
(270) 726-2737
dfgriff@yahoo.com
www.geocities.com/dfgriff

A take on politics and current events—local, national and international.

RANDOM LENGTHS NEWS
P.O. Box 731
San Pedro, CA 90733-0731
(310) 519-1442
Fax: (310) 832-1000
Randomlengths90731@yahoo.com

REAL SOCIETY
A publication of RealNews Service
P.O. Box 773
Coupeville, WA 98239
(519) 893-5321
Fax: (519) 893-0735

coho@whidbey.net
www.realnews.org

An in depth, no excuses look into the environmental issues of Vancouver's Salish Sea.

RENO NEWS & REVIEW
708 N Center St.
Reno, NV 89501
(702) 324-4440
Fax: (702) 324-4572
newsreview.com

RIVERFRONT TIMES
6358 Delmar Blvd., Suite 200
St. Louis, MO 63130-4719
(314) 615-6666
Fax: (314) 615-6655
rftstl.com

ROCKY MOUNTAIN MEDIA WATCH
P.O. Box 18858
Denver, CO 80218
(303) 832-7558
Fax: (303) 832-7558
www.imagepage.com/rmmw

RUSSIAN RIVER TIMES
P.O. Box 573
Monte Rio, CA 95462
(707) 869-2010
rrtimes@sonic.net

A twice-monthly paper of the North Bay area.

SACRAMENTO COMMENT
1114 21st Street
Sacramento, CA 95814
scotts@sl.net

Reportage and commentary on Sacramento regional and California state politics, as well as general criticism. Straight forward, nonjargonistic writing with a sense of humor.

SACRAMENTO NEWS & REVIEW
1015 20th Street
Sacramento, CA 95814
(916) 498-1234
Fax: (916) 498-7910
NewsReview@aol.com
www.newsreview.com

SACRAMENTO OBSERVER, THE
2330 Alhambra Blvd.
P.O. Box 209
Sacramento, CA 95817
(916) 452-4781
info@sacobserver.com
www.sacobserver.com

The most honored black newspaper in America.

SALT LAKE CITY WEEKLY
60 West 400 South
Salt Lake City, UT 84101
(801) 575-7003
Fax: (801) 575-6106
jsaltas@slweekly.com
www.slweekly.com

SAN ANTONIO CURRENT
1500 N St. Mary's St.
San Antonio, TX 78215
(210) 227-0044
Fax: (210) 227-7733
www.sacurrent.com

San Antonio's progressive weekly newpaper.

SAN DIEGO READER
1703 India St.
San Diego, CA 92101
(619) 235-3000
Fax: (619) 231-0489
hrosen@sdreader.com
www.sdreader.com

SAN FRANCISCO BAY GUARDIAN
520 Hampshire
San Francisco, CA 94110-1417
(415) 255-3100
Fax: (415) 255-8762
sfguardian@aol.com
www.sfbg.com

"The best of the Bay...every week!"

SAN FRANCISCO BAY TIMES
3410 19th Street
San Francisco, CA 94110
(415) 626-0260
Fax: (415) 626-0987
sfbaytimes@aol.co,

A gay/lesbian/bi/trans newspaper and events calendar of the Bay area.

SAN FRANCISCO BUSINESS TIMES
275 Battery St., Suite 940
San Francisco, CA 94111
(415) 989-2522
Fax: (415) 398-2494
sanfrancisco.bcentral.com
www.sanfrancisco.bcentral.com

SAN FRANCISCO FRONTLINES
3311 Mission St., Suite 135
San Francisco, CA 94110
(415) 452-9992
Fax: (415) 643-8581
progress@ix.netcom.com
www.sf-frontlines.com

A San Francisco Bay area progressive monthly.

SANTA BARBARA INDEPENDENT
1221 State St., Suite 200
Santa Barbara, CA 93101
(805) 965-5205
Fax: (805) 965-5518
www.independent.com

SANTA FE REPORTER
132 E Marcy St.
Santa Fe, NM 87501
(505) 988-5541
Fax: (505) 988-5348
71632.223@compuserve.com

SEATTLE SKANNER NEWSPAPER
P.O. Box 94473
Seattle, WA 98124-6773
(206) 233-9888
Fax: (206) 233-9795
theskanner2@earthlink.net
www.theskanner.com

An African-American weekly.

SEATTLE WEEKLY
1008 Western Ave., Suite 300
Seattle, WA 98104
(206) 623-0500
Fax: (206) 467-4338
editorial@seattleweekly.com
www.seattleweekly.com

SEEN MAGAZINE
Published by Black Slickety Press
345 Riverview, Lower Level 1
Wichita, KS 67203
(316) 269-4389
Fax: (316) 269-9400
carmody@feist.com
www.galaxycorp.com/cmkrc

The monthly journal of Midwestern
infraculture.

SEMINOLE TRIBUNE
6300 Stirling Rd.
Hollywood, FL 33024
(954) 967-3416
Fax: (954) 967-3482
www.seminoletribe.com

The newspaper of the Seminole
tribe of Florida.

SEVEN DAYS
P.O. Box 1164
Burlington, VT 05402
(802) 864-5684
Fax: (802) 865-1015
sevenday@together.net
www.sevendaysvt.com

SF WEEKLY
185 Berry St., Suite 3800
San Francisco, CA 94107
(415) 541-0700
Fax: (415) 777-1839
www.sfweekly.com

**SHARE GUIDE: THE HOLISTIC
HEALTH MAGAZINE**
P.O. Box 420
Graton, CA 95444
share@shareguide.com
www.shareguide.com

A free holistic health magazine and
resource directory focusing on alternative medicine, personal growth
and environmental issues.

SHEPHERD EXPRESS
413 North 2nd Street, Suite 150
Milwaukee, WI 53203
(414) 276-2222
Fax: (414) 276-3312
postmaster@shepherd-express.com
www.shepherd-express.com

SHO-BAN NEWS
P.O. Box 900
Fort Hall, ID 83203
(208) 478-3701
www.shobannews.com

The Shoshone-Bannock tribes'
weekly.

SONOMA VALLEY VOICE
P.O. Box 907
Boyes Hot Springs, CA 95416
(707) 996-9678
Fax: (707) 996-8859
sonomavalleyvoice@vom.com

A quarterly of alternative news and
opinion.

SOUTHERN COMMUNITIES
P.O. Box 121133
Nashville, TN 37212-1133
(615) 297-2629
www.southerncommunities.com

STRANGER, THE
1202 E Pike St., Suite 1225
Seattle, WA 98122
(206) 323-7101
Fax: (206) 325-4865
www.thestranger.com

STREET NEWS
144-46 76th Avenue
K.G.H., NY 11367
(718) 268-5165
streetnews@othersides.com
www.othersides.com/streetnews.htm

STREET SPIRIT
65 9th Street
San Francisco, CA 94103-1401
(415) 565-0201
Fax: (415) 565-0204
spirit@afsc-pmr.org

Justice news and homeless blues
from the San Francisco Bay area.

STREETWISE CHICAGO
1331 S Michigan Ave.
Chicago, IL 60605
(312) 554-0060
Fax: (312) 554-0770
jstrong@streetwise.org
www.streetwise.com

StreetWise Chicago is a weekly
alternative street paper sold by the
homeless around Chicago.

SUN REPORTER, THE
1791 Bancroft Ave.
San Francisco, CA 94124
(415) 671-1000
Fax: (415) 931-0214
www.sunreporter.com

The original African-American weekly in San Francisco.

SYRACUSE NEW TIMES
1415 W Genesee St.
Syracuse, NY 13204-2156
(315) 422-7011
Fax: (315) 422-1721
menglish@syracusenewtimes.com
newtimes.rway.com

TENNESSEE TRIBUNE, THE
1501 Jefferson St.
Nashville, TN 37208
(615) 321-3268
Fax: (615) 321-0409
Ten37208@aol.com
www.tennesseetribune.com

An African-American weekly.

**TRANSPORTATION
ALTERNATIVES**
115 West 30th Street, #1207
New York, NY 10001
(212) 629-8080
Fax: (212) 629-8334
info@transalt.org
www.transalt.org

News and advocacy for greater use

of human-powered transportation in New York City.

TRI-STATE DEFENDER
124 G.E. Patterson
Memphis, TN 38103
(901) 523-1818
Fax: (901) 523-1520
tsdefend@bellsouth.net

An African-American weekly.

TUCSON WEEKLY
P.O. Box 2429
Tucson, AZ 85702
(520) 792-3630
Fax: (520) 792-2096
sales@tucsonweekly.com
www.tucsonweekly.com

URBAN ECOLOGY
414 13th Street, Suite 500
Oakland, CA 94612
(510) 251-6330
Fax: (510) 251-2117
urbanecology@urbanecology.org
www.urbanecology.org

Urban Ecology envisions, designs and plans cities to support a healthy natural environment, a multicultural and thriving community, and an innovative and vigorous local economy.

VILLAGE VOICE, THE
36 Cooper Square
New York, NY 10003
(212) 475-3300
Fax: (212) 475-8944
info@villagevoice.com
www.villagevoice.com

A weekly newspaper covering
regional, national and international
affairs from a New York perspective.

VOICE OF THE WILD SISKIYOU
P.O. Box 220
Cave Junction, OR 97523
(541) 592-4459
Fax: (541) 592-2653
project@siskiyou.org
www.siskiyou.org

Quarterly newsletter of the Siskiyou
Regional Education Project.

VOIR MONTRÉAL
4130 Saint-Denis
Montréal, QC H2W 2M5
Canada
(514) 848-0805
Fax: (514) 848-9004
www.voir.ca

VOIR QUÉBEC
470 rue de la Couronne
Québec, QC G1K 6G2
(418) 522-7777
Fax: (418) 522-7779
www.voir.ca

VOZ FRONTERIZA
Dept. 0077 UCSD
9500 Gilman Dr.
La Jolla, CA 92093-0077
(619) 534-3616
burn.ucsd.edu/~cpa/vozfronteriza/vo
zfronterizaindex.html

A quarterly Chicano-Mexicano student newspaper founded in 1975.

WASHINGTON AFRO-AMERICAN
1612 14th Street NW, 2nd floor
Washington, DC 20001
(202) 332-0080
ammanuelm@afroam.org
www.afro.com

WASHINGTON CITY PAPER
2390 Champlain St., NW
Washington, DC 20009
(202) 332-2100
Fax: (202) 462-8323
mail@washcp.com
www.washingtoncitypaper.com

WASHINGTON FREE PRESS
PMB #178, 1463 East Republican
Seattle, WA 98112
(206) 860-5290
freepress@scn.org
www.washingtonfreepress.org

The *Washington Free Press* reports
the underreported events of the
Northwest, specializing in labor
and environmental topics. It pres-

ents bimonthly progressive news from Seattle and throughout Washington.

WASHINGTON INFORMER
3117 M.L. King Ave. SE
Washington, DC 20032
(202) 561-4100
Fax: (202) 574-3785
washington.informer@verizon.net

An African-American weekly.

WAUSAU CITY PAGES
P.O. Box 942
Wausau, WI 54402-0942
(715) 845-5171
Fax: (715) 848-5887
citypages@pcpros.net

WE THE PEOPLE
Published by the Redwood Empire
Lesbian, Gay, and Bisexual
Education Project
P.O. Box 8218
Santa Rosa, CA 95407
(707) 573-8896
WTP Pub@aol.com

WEEKLY ALIBI
2118 Central Ave. SE, Suite 151
Albuquerque, NM 87106-4004
(505) 268-8111
Fax: (505) 256-9651
desert.net/alibi

WEEKLY PLANET
1310 E 9th Avenue
Tampa, FL 33605
(813) 248-8888
Fax: (813) 248-9999
ed@weeklyplanet.com
www.weeklyplanet.com/current

WESTWORD
969 Broadway
P.O. Box 597
Denver, CO 80217
(303) 296-7744
Fax: (303) 296-5416
www.westword.com

WILD CALIFORNIA
Published by the Environmental
Protection Information Center(EPIC)
P.O. Box 397
Garberville, CA 95542
(707) 923-2931
Fax: (707) 923-4210
epic@wildcalifornia.org
www.wildcalifornia.org

WILLAMETTE WEEK
822 SW 10th Avenue
Portland, OR 97205
(503) 243-2122
Fax: (503) 243-1115
www.wweek.com

An alternative weekly newspaper serving the Portland area.

WIND RIVER NEWS
332 Main St.
Lander, WY 82520
(307) 332-2323
Fax: (307) 332-9332
newsdept@wyoming.com

This weekly newspaper serves the members of the Shoshone and Arapaho tribes on the Wind River Indian Reservation and across the Rocky Mountain region.

WOMEN'S VOICES (SONOMA COUNTY)
Published by Women's Support Network
P.O. Box 4448
Santa Rosa, CA 95402-4448
(707) 575-5654
wv@monitor.net

WORCESTER MAGAZINE
172 Shrewsbury St.
Worcester, MA 01604
(508) 755-8004
Fax: (508) 755-4734
editorial@worcestermag.com
www.worcestermag.com

A weekly alternative newspaper.

INDEX
ALPHABETICAL

INDEX
BY SECTION

REGIONAL PUBLICATIONS